D1068718

Organizational Resilience

ORGANIZATIONAL RESILIENCE

How Learning Sustains Organizations in Crisis, Disaster, and Breakdown

D. Christopher Kayes

OXFORD
UNIVERSITY PRESS

OXFORD
UNIVERSITY PRESS

Oxford University Press is a department of the University of
Oxford. It furthers the University's objective of excellence in research,
scholarship, and education by publishing worldwide.

Oxford   New York
Auckland   Cape Town   Dar es Salaam   Hong Kong   Karachi
Kuala Lumpur   Madrid   Melbourne   Mexico City   Nairobi
New Delhi   Shanghai   Taipei   Toronto

With offices in
Argentina   Austria   Brazil   Chile   Czech Republic   France   Greece
Guatemala   Hungary   Italy   Japan   Poland   Portugal   Singapore
South Korea   Switzerland   Thailand   Turkey   Ukraine   Vietnam

Oxford is a registered trademark of Oxford University Press
in the UK and certain other countries.

Published in the United States of America by
Oxford University Press
198 Madison Avenue, New York, NY 10016

Library of Congress Cataloging-in-Publication Data
Kayes, D. Christopher.
Organizational resilience : how learning sustains organizations in crisis, disaster, and breakdown /
by D. Christopher Kayes.
pages cm
Includes bibliographical references and index.
ISBN 978-0-19-979105-7
1. Organizational learning.   2. Organizational resilience.   3. Crisis management.   I. Title.
HD58.82.K393 2015
658.3'124—dc23
2014039236

9 8 7 6 5 4 3 2 1
Printed in the United States of America
on acid-free paper

CONTENTS

PREFACE

In the complex and dynamic world of organizations, learning and adaptation become the central activity of organizations for building organizational resilience. Despite the importance of learning, organizational observers continue to struggle for a satisfactory explanation for why organizations learn and why organizational learning can break down. This book provides new insights into how organizations learn by exploring how organizations, and those in them, learn from their experience.

Unlike most discussions of organizational resilience, which focus on system-wide problems, *Organizational Resilience: How Learning Sustains Organizations in Crisis, Disaster, and Breakdown* focuses on the role of individual experience as the source of learning in organizations. Individual experience, the book shows, sets the stage for learning across the organization, including the individual, team, and system levels of interaction. The book expands on well-known theories of learning put forth by the likes of philosopher John Dewey, learning theorist David Kolb, and others to show their relevance for building resilience.

The book offers new insights into building organizational resilience through learning. It looks at how a high capacity for learning sustains organizations. For example, commercial aviation in the United States is one of the most complex and reliable systems in history, with an accident rate of less than .05%. Occasionally, however, accidents do occur, like the Air France 447 disaster in 2009, which killed all passengers and crew. A review of the events leading to the crash reveals a possible breakdown in learning from gaps in training, a weak team-leadership structure, the inability of the crew to adequately shift from a performance mode to a learning mode, and a system of error detection that failed to inform the cockpit crew of a common equipment failure.

The book also offers insights into how normally helpful organizational processes, like goal setting and evidence-based decision making, can threaten resilience. For example, citing a train derailment and a seemingly ill-conceived emergency-medical-care standard as examples, the author concludes that many systematic failures in organizations are due to unrealistic performance standards that motivate organizations to push systems to their operational, psychological, and financial limits. By drawing on well-known business breakdowns like those of Enron, Lehman Brothers, and Kodak, the book explains how organizational routines and the orientation of organizational members are often among the biggest barriers to building resilience.

Most important, the book shows how organizations build the capacity to learn from mistakes and failures when they view breakdowns as a normal part of the learning process. The book reveals a counterintuitive claim: Breakdowns themselves are necessary but often painful precursors to learning, and initial breakdowns in learning can fuel an overall improvement in how an organization functions. Examples of organizational resilience include the corporate transformation in the aftermath of the Exxon Valdez oil spill, changes in decision making that took place in the Kennedy administration in the aftermath of the Bay of Pigs debacle, and changes in how elements of the U.S. intelligence community review knowledge in light of the failure to accurately estimate the presence of weapons of mass destruction in Iraq. Each of these examples shows how long-term operations can be improved when breakdowns in learning are perceived as "educative" experiences that lead to continuous learning.

The book is divided into three main sections. Section I explains how individuals learn from experience and outlines the basis for learning. This section describes how individual experience is translated into organizational learning through routines, identity, and culture. Section II presents various ways that failure has been discussed and proposes an alternative to failure—the breakdown of learning. The section goes on to describe how normally helpful organizational routines, such as optimism, goal setting, and rational thinking, can actually induce the breakdown of learning. Section III presents several examples of how to learn to become more resilient in the face of catastrophic breakdown.

ALPHABETICAL LIST OF CASE STUDIES AND EXAMPLES

INTRODUCTION: LEARNING AS THE SOURCE OF RESILIENCE

A consideration of resilience in organizations begins by asking questions like the following:

- What can be learned from organizations as they experience isolated failures and breakdowns?
- How do organizations fail to learn from past experiences and repeat mistakes, despite making efforts at lessons learned?
- When do normally helpful organizational practices, such as goal setting and systematic decision making, become harmful?

Answers to these questions emerge from looking more carefully at learning in organizations. Learning, better than other organizational activities, explains how organizations sustain resilience in the face of disaster, crisis, and breakdown. More importantly, the break down of learning better explains what, how, and when organizations fail. Without learning, even the simplest of organizational processes come under threat. When learning stalls, organizations underperform and face the risk of breakdown.

The book proposes that the breakdown of learning contributes to and is responsible for many organizational failures. Learning from experience is a key to organizational functioning, and when learning from experience breaks down, organizations become vulnerable. A better understanding of organizational failure comes from understanding learning from experience in organizations as a multifaceted process. Of particular interest is an understanding of learning from the perspective of those experiencing the breakdown itself. Understanding how those within organizations learn from events and how those individuals experience failure provides important clues to organizational resilience.

The book highlights important factors associated with learning in organizations and how learning can help organizations become more resilient as they prevent, respond to, and recover from organizational failure. Although the terms "failure," "crisis," and "disaster" are often used interchangeably in discussions of organizations, the term "breakdown" is suggested as an alternative because it emphasizes that the natural process of organizational learning has stalled. The breakdown of learning is explored in policy, government, business, and healthcare. Recounting the events from Air France Flight 944 breakdown and the breakdown in organizational intelligence associated with the search for WMD in Iraq can be instructive about the breakdown of learning. Examples from government, transportation, self-improvement, finance, and healthcare provide details of how learning serves as the primary force for organizational survival, and offers warnings on how the breakdown of learning threaten even the most successful companies. More importantly, these events can instruct on how to rebuild learning in light of its breakdown.

A visit to 1960s New Orleans and the search for deadly bacteria illustrate the need for new ways of thinking about organizational failure and how learning from experience offers an alternative mode of analyzing such failures.

THE SEARCH FOR BUBONIC PLAGUE IN NEW ORLEANS

George was sweating. Nothing made him more nervous than handling the rats. In the sewers and back alleys of New Orleans in the 1960s, the rats grew as big as cats. They grew muscled, feisty, and smelly from their feasts of garbage. They also served as bushel baskets of disease. A man from the New Orleans animal control unit brought these rats to George and his co-workers. The man himself looked muscled, feisty, and smelly. He brought creaky cages into the laboratory and clumsily dropped them on the lab floor so that cages piled up like packages waiting to be opened.

At first, George followed the recommended procedures, as outlined in the lab manual, when handling a rat. He relied on a set of steel tongs, provided by the lab, to grab the rodent by the neck. He hoisted the rat, crane-like, out of the cage and into a large clear glass jar. He deliberately released the rat into the jar, quickly covering it with a steel lid, closing off the escape route before the rat could jump out the top of the jar. In the final step, George applied ether through a tiny hole in the lid as he watched the rat meet a quick and peaceful death.

On one occasion, things did not go so well. It was hot and humid in New Orleans, and handling rats that potentially carried disease made George nervous, and the sweat made the tongs slippery. The tongs slipped out of his hands. The rat escaped the clutches of the tongs and scurried across the floor. It becomes a race between man and rat. George knew there had to be a better way to handle rats than what had been prescribed in the manual. Standard operating procedures had to be adjusted. To overcome the problem of the escaping rat, George devised a method that was far more efficient and less prone to error. He simply approached the cage brought to him by the animal control unit manager, wrapped the original cage with duct tape, making sure no air holes existed, and dripped the ether directly into the airtight cage. This way, George never needed to open the cage, eliminating any possible escape route. The method proved resilient. Duct tape is inexpensive and can be reused over and over again.

Once the rat was dead, the repugnant work began: placing the rat on a steel gurney, cutting the rat open, and performing tests to determine if the rat carried infectious diseases. George's nervous sweating was warranted, because many diseases rested in the fleas that traveled on rats. Should one of the fleas be infected and then hop onto George's arm, he would likely be infected himself. The provoking agent: bubonic plague. If he went untreated, he himself might become a carrier of the disease, infecting others around him as he hacked and coughed the deadly bacteria into the air. Working infectious disease duty was without question the most unappealing work of the aspiring biologist.

George provides an example of the importance of learning from experience in organizations. As George dissected and diagnosed each rat, he was helping to identify a small threat before it turned into a full-blown crisis. Despite the inevitable nerves, George might identify an early strain of the plague and avert the spread of disease across New Orleans. George, our biology graduate student, was in search of more than his doctorate in biology; he sought evidence of bubonic plague, a bacterium associated with unsanitary and close living quarters among humans. To successfully contain the epidemic, he needs to identify a threat early and then to take action before the threat spreads. George was learning from experience.

RATS IN A JAR VERSUS RATS IN A CAGE

George's work shows how learning from experience leads to learning in the larger system. Learning from experience occurred as George modified his approach to rat collection and transfer. George began using a new protocol—we will call it a rat-in-a-cage protocol—because it lowered the chances of a rat escaping and thus potential exposure to disease. The original protocol—we will call it the rat-in-a-jar protocol—introduced the possibility of escape. In a very simple way, George relied on his experience and identified a more effective method to improve the diagnostic processes. Through the systematic gathering, processing, and observation of rats, learning was being built into the health system.

One reason that George's work with rats is interesting is that it illustrates the processes by which organizations rely on learning to improve everyday practice. Learning requires adapting and modifying practices based on insight and experimentation. George's work also illustrates how learning is embedded within the routines of organizational learning. Whether considering the protocol, the specific knowledge of disease, or even the search specifically for bubonic plague, each of these aspects shows the embedded context of learning.

LEARNING IN ORGANIZATIONS GROUNDED
IN HUMAN EXPERIENCE

Working directly with the rats alerted George to a greater vulnerability. Existing protocols for rat handling led to the introduction of a problem: the loose rat. Learning wasn't limited to what George thought about the situation (e.g., cognitive factors) or to the interaction with technology that led him to adjust the protocols (e.g., human technology interaction), but included George's openness to new approaches and his experimentation. The basis of George's work was grounded in human experience. These experiences involved a complex set of past actions, emotions, future expectations, and specific and general knowledge about the way the world works. A look at George's experience with the rats sets us on a course to better understand the connection between individual experience and its role in learning in organizations. Luckily, for both George and the people of New Orleans, he never found a rat with anything like the plague.

Throughout this book, I enlist specific events to illustrate the nature of learning from experience in organizations. Events can take the form of cases, stories, and formal studies, but always include accounts of what happened in the course of a breakdown. By recounting events, the book offers detailed descriptions of learning and invites interpretation and reinterpretation of the events in light of emerging organizational concepts (March, Sproull, & Tamuz, 1991). Events move the reader closer to experiencing the events as they occurred, putting the reader, in some sense, in the middle of the action. The retrospective reflection on experience often yields new insights into what may have been experienced in real time.

By looking closely at specific events, we might uncover the *experience* associated with the breakdown of learning from the perspective of those embedded in the situation. Understanding these experiences we begin to enter the world of unbelievability. Goffman (1959) described unbelievability with a question, 'How could we have been so unreasonable about what we thought we saw before, now that we see the outcome?' The question suggests that to understand why decisions were made, actions taken, and lessons learned or not learned is largely a matter of context and perspective—the immediate experiences of the moment. Unbelievability, then, suggests that what is learned is not a given but is constructed from a particular set of events and reconstructed differently with each new iteration of the learning process (Clegg, Courpasson, & Phillips, 2006, p. 119).

In one set of events, I recount the disaster of Air France Flight 447 that seemingly fell from the sky without notice. Reading about a crash is difficult, but the events reveal how easy it is to discount the role of experience in an age that increasingly relies on technology. Reviewing what the pilots did and did not experience provides a new insight into the factors that led to the breakdown of learning inside the cockpit, despite having access to the latest technology. In fact, the events reveal that reliance on technology at the expense of experience contributed to the disaster as the pilots failed to effectively shift from routine to novel operating procedures in the face of an unfamiliar environment. Whether the failure resulted from a lack of experience, poor training, or lack of organizational coordination, the events reveal the fragility of an organization when demands supersede the capacity of the organizational members to learn.

In another set of events, I explore the search for and eventual reconsideration of weapons of mass destruction in Iraq. These events make evident important links between organizational intelligence theory and practice. Although events associated with the search for WMD are widely cited and specific details about them are widely available, the book provides a concise history and analysis of the events that seeks to place them in the literature on learning, organizational breakdown, and decision making. The events take place primarily in 2003 and 2004, but history, as we will see, plays an important role in shaping what lessons we learn. The U.S. government intelligence service serves as an example for how organizational politics, coordination, and culture can both enhance and inhibit learning. The events provide insights into how organizational and psychological concepts, such as learning, can be helpful in understanding policy decisions (Tetlock & Mellers, 2011). The strong conviction held by the members of the intelligence community that Iraq maintained an active biological weapons production program provide a window into organizational learning and its breakdown that are akin to the insights gained from historical policy events such as the Challenger disaster, the Bay of Pigs, and the Cuban missile crisis. Specifically, the events revealed that organizational politics, lack of coordination, and past experiences often lead to miseducative experience. Unquestioned routines can lead to inaccurate, but not unexpected, assessments of a situation. The organization's concern with performance rather than learning contributed to a miseducative experience, and despite dissenting views within the intelligence community, the community rallied around the dominant viewpoint.

ORGANIZATION OF THE BOOK

The book offers an explanation for how people learn in organizations, but more importantly, it identifies how organizations become compromised when learning breaks down. The book contains three Sections:

Section I argues for a better understanding of the role that experience plays in learning in organizations by outlining elements of a theory of experience and learning in organizations. The section offers a description of learning in organizations that falls along two dimensions. One dimension shows a distinction between a learning and performance orientation. A second dimension considers differences in learning required for routine versus novel operating environments. Taken together, these dimensions provide a framework to distinguish between four interrelated modes of learning from experience in organizations: evidence-based learning, direct experience, counter experience, and exploration.

The idea that experience is the basis for learning in organizations grows out of the pragmatic philosophy of John Dewey (1938), whose notion of learning from experience has been widely adopted (Kolb, 1984). Despite the wide recognition that experience plays a role in learning, a comprehensive consideration of learning from experience as it applies to organizations has yet to be realized. Drawing on the works of Dewey and Kolb, three aspects of experience—habits, emotions, and cognitions—serve as the basis for learning in organizations and how background knowledge, know-how, and preparation enhance experiential learning. This section also addresses the critics of learning from experience and argues that many of the critics have missed the point of what it means to learn from experience (e.g., March, 2011).

Section II applies concepts of learning from experience to organizational processes and explores several different characterizations of failure in organizations. The experiential approach to learning in organizations also offers a new perspective on organizational failure. Reviewing key approaches to failure, including psychological, sociological, human error, and high-reliability system approaches, the first chapter in this section considers the limitations of each approach. Irving Janis's concept of groupthink provides a starting point for understanding the limitations of how we currently view failure in organizations. The chapter concludes that learning, in conjunction with other perspectives, provides new insights into organizational resilience. The study of organizations is ripe with discussions of failure. Oftentimes, failure is associated with the inability of an organization to respond appropriately to external circumstances that eventually result in organizational collapse (Christensen, 2000). This section builds on this idea but by providing insights into how experience and learning play a role in organizational collapse. In the end, the section offers a new conceptualization of organizational breakdown based on how organizations learn, or often fail to learn from experience.

An alternative way to think about organizational failure is proposed: the breakdown of learning. Chapter 5 describes different aspects of learning from experience and how the breakdown of learning can emerge from a failure to learn from experience. Rather than consider organizational problems as failures, the following pages argue that many organizational challenges result from the breakdown of learning. Learning breaks down because experience is often enlisted to teach the wrong lessons or in some cases offers no lesson at all.

In subsequent chapters, Section II introduces several unlikely threats to learning. Under certain conditions, goal setting and the pursuit of goals limit learning as goal-setting efforts tend to focus individuals and organizations on performance-oriented, rather than learning-oriented, activities. Examples of the destructive side of goals include the 4-h target in emergency medicine in the United Kingdom (Hardern, 2012) and the early push to reach the moon by

NASA. A look at Enron, one of the largest corporate collapses in history, proposes that several popular management practices, including pay for performance and other reward systems, unsuspectingly contribute to the breakdown of learning in organizations. The 2008 financial crisis in general, and the bankruptcy of Lehman Brothers in particular, serve as examples of the breakdown of learning. The section also considers problems with traditional approaches to decision making, including the rational approaches and the behavioral economics approaches. An alternative model of decision making is proposed that considers tensions that emerge during the experiential learning process.

Section III integrates several of the ideas, models, and terms offered in the book, beginning with an extended case study of what has been called the greatest intelligence failure in a generation: the misinterpretation of intelligence of weapons of mass destruction in Iraq in 2002 and 2003. This case study in chapter 9 provides a narrative approach to understanding organizational breakdown and the early stages of rebuilding in the face of breakdown, illustrating some of the challenges to learning faced by knowledge-based organizations. The final chapter provides more case studies, including a discussion of how certain players in the oil and gas industry have recovered from catastrophic failure to build organizations that rely on continuous learning. The book concludes by drawing on these and other events to show how organizations can begin to rebuild learning in the aftermath of breakdown. The conclusion offers future directions for the study of organizational learning and outlines ways that the study of organizational resilience can inform practice.

The book challenges the conventional wisdom that says learning in organizations is mainly about analyzing market data, conducting competitive analysis, recognizing shifting markets, and responding to emerging technologies. As a process of gathering and processing new knowledge, learning is infused with emotion, is cognitively challenging, and is present in routine actions. In the end, learning offers improved organizational performance.

EXPERIENCE, LEARNING, RESILIENCE

Consider George, the young biologist, once again. Like George's initial understanding of how to handle rats, existing conceptualizations of learning in organizations remain inadequate. We lack a deeper understanding of the role that experience plays in learning and how this learning is translated into organizational processes. When individuals in organizations are open to new experiences, reflect on successes and failures, update their perspective, and take calculated risks and experimentation, they learn. Organizations that cultivate learning from experience build organizational resilience.

Experience as the Source of Learning in Organizations

CHAPTER 1

Learning from Experience

THE CENTRALITY OF LEARNING FROM EXPERIENCE

When most people think of learning, they think about sitting in a classroom listening to a lecture, memorizing lists or facts, or practicing a new skill for work or recreation. These are all activities people do when they learn, but this book focuses on a different type of learning: learning from experience. The learning addressed in this book involves reflecting upon, drawing lessons from, and taking action upon prior experience. Learning also describes how individuals within organizations learn tasks, develop and change organizational norms, and conduct the daily routines that are a part of how organizations function. Learning is both formal and informal, as it occurs when individuals sit in training sessions, but also when they observe procedures to identify ways to improve upon these procedures. Learning occurs as a natural part of human interaction, and learning is deliberately built into organizational functioning. Learning is a natural, but often unrecognized, function of organizational life and is essential for normal organizational operation. When learning breaks down, organizations become vulnerable to change, shifts in procedures, and small errors.

The experiential basis of learning is contrasted to more rationalistic approaches, such as the approach to learning advocated by James March (2011). March described learning from experience as the result of "intelligence gained from converting instances of experience into possible understandings of the world" (1302 of 1754). Despite his helpful definition of experiential learning, March is no supporter of the notion that people in organizations learn from experience. He believes that experience provides a poor substitute for objective data because experience is a kind of trope, a deception. In addition, his view is that the lessons learned from experience lack truth and are too flexible and that learning from experience results in lessons that are simply shaped by our *preconceived desire to maintain existing beliefs*. For March, experience is not to be trusted because the "vivid and compelling" stories that emerge from experience result in interpretations that are seductive rather than deductive. March laments the popularity that the notion "learning from experience" has gained in recent years (citing Kayes, 2002 and Kolb, 1984 as examples). Many advocate that learning in organizations is based on experience, but March believes the success of experiential learning is born from a kind of deception. Learning from experience has seduced organizations into adopting experiential learning practices, he believes, because those who adopt the notion have effectively been duped by the emotional content of the cause. Learning from experience, accordingly, constitutes a kind of organizational "folk intelligence" that results in only weak interpretations of reality because these interpretations emerge from our existing frames of reference and the samples of experience we draw on are far too few to be of any real use.

March's argument against learning from experience emerges from assumptions he makes about what it means to learn. His consideration of learning is both rationalistic and stilted. March believes that experience is too complex to result in clear cause-and-effect relationships, that organizations are too full of complexity, and that experience is clouded by too much noise to be of use. Experience is a kind of imagination rather than hard cold evidence. Ultimately, experience is too self-centered and too socially embedded to serve as the basis of objective learning. Experience, he says, is like history: open to interpretation. In contrast to learning from experience, March advocates a kind of hypothesis testing that is born from repeated trial and error, performed and recorded methodically. Organizational intelligence, according to March, is gained through a kind of ongoing laboratory study of events. In his embrace of organizational rationality, March has joined a renewed attempt among scholars to legitimize forms of learning that have been blessed by organizational scholars as consistent with procedures of "science."

March has joined the chorus here, advocating for evidence-based learning. Even as March places much emphasis on evidence as the basis of learning, he is not able to provide direct evidence of the value of direct evidence over direct experience. March seems to track closely the comments made by Day (2010), who concludes that learning from experience is too difficult to measure because individuals and their observers can never be sure if learning occurred, what was learned, and if people are even aware of what they learned. Day compares learning from experience to an unstructured, undisciplined, even wild process, in which learning is largely at the mercy of a complex hairy beast known as the organization. Instead, Day enlists the literature on expertise (e.g., Ericsson, 2009) to suggest that the same rules that apply to learning well-structured problems, such as chess, can easily be applied to learning more complex tasks such as leadership. Yet, Day still insists on considering the skills associated with chess and other domain-specific skills as different from those associated with leadership. Nonetheless, both March and Day make a common conceptual error when they mistake "experience" itself from the processes associated with "learning from experience" (see Kayes & Kayes, 2011). Experience alone may produce only noise, but learning from experience, when done deliberately, can lead to insights, meaning, and judgment.

Reagans, Argote, and Brooks (2005) in their study of surgery teams may provide a healthy response to those skeptical of measuring how individuals learn from experience in organizations. The researchers looked at various types of experiences, including individual experience and experiences working together in a team, to identify how experience may or may not have impacted performance outcomes in hip and knee replacement surgery. They concluded that experience does matter. The more experience an organization has at performing hip and knee replacements, the more quickly the procedure can be performed. In particular, the more experience a person has working on a particular team with a particular group of team members, the more efficient the surgical team becomes. By working together as part of a team, team members increase their knowledge of others' expertise and also increase knowledge and skills at coordinating behaviors. Although team and organizational experience matter, individual experience, interestingly, had a negative impact on performance time, at least initially.

According to their study, the actual relationship between performance and experience was an inverted U shape, in which process loss initially occurred but process gains were realized over time. For the first five surgeries, each procedure took longer to complete, but after five surgeries, medical professionals began to see an improvement in their operational time. The finding that early procedures don't realize process gains but only losses is only surprising when considering the more traditional definition of learning and the standard learning curve. Efficiency approaches to the learning curve depict learning as a positive function of performance over time. In complex environments, however, an inverted U may be expected. Performance is likely to suffer because early in a team's formation, individuals identify areas for improvement, spend time learning team dynamics, and engage in learning that is not directly related to direct performance. Although the activities seems ancillary, they are important for the longer term performance of the team. There is also a broader theoretical implication that more experience in certain routines will lead to better performance after an initial period which is characterized by lower performance. The early performance lag on the road to success was highlighted by Reagans's study. Said another way, early failures may simply be the first signal of resilience. Figure 1.1 illustrates a revision of the traditional learning curve that includes the preoperational considerations captured by the study of surgery teams.

The critique of experiential learning is largely a philosophical one, as the arguments put forth by critics of experience fail to provide direct evidence that evidence-based learning is more effective than experience-based learning. Even economists have begun to embraced a more comprehensive understanding of learning by accepting both the quantitative and qualitative aspects of learning. The qualitative aspects of learning often involve "emotions," whereas the more quantitative aspects embrace "facts." Daniel Kahneman (2011) has spent his

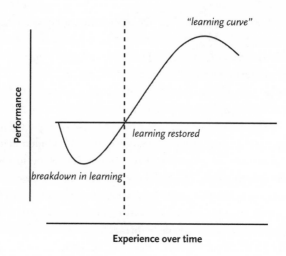

Figure 1.1:
Preoperational zone of organizational learning.

professional life trying to understand how (and why) people make decisions that don't conform to rational thinking. For Kahneman and others in the behavioral economics camp, learning should be linked to rational processes, namely, accurately calculating probabilities and making decisions based on those probabilities. Kahneman has come to embrace a more holistic approach to decision making that involves two distinct forms of decision making—which correspond roughly to two different forms of learning. Fast decision making involves immediate response, what managers refer to as intuition or "gut feelings." Slow decision making is the deliberate, step-by-step, calculated form of decision making that we associate with rational, planned decision-making efforts. Kahneman seems to be embracing a need for both types of learning: an experience-based learning and a rational, evidence-based form of learning. The next section of this chapter considers how individuals in organizations learn from experience by exploring the roots of experience itself.

THE NATURE OF EXPERIENCE

What is experience? Scharf (1998) offered two distinct characteristics of experience that help to answer this question. The first characteristic of experience connotes a direct and distinct event that can be located in time and place. Thus, an experience involves "living through" or "participating in" a time and place (p. 276). The participation characteristic of experience implies a point in history, an event that has occurred. It implies experience that is shaped by culture, environment, social relationships, cultural understanding, expectations, and aspirations (p. 271). This public aspect of experience is always mediated by the available cultural tools at hand in the form of words, symbols, tools, and so on. The second characteristic of experience is an awareness or consciousness of the self and surroundings of the event, which connotes a private act. This private characteristic of experience implies a subjectivity, an emotion, or an internal event that may be distinct from its external events. Although Scharf viewed the private characteristic of experience as problematic, the private aspect of experience is important for learning because it is linked to intuition (see, for example, Klein, 1999) and tacit knowledge (Polyani, 1974).

Whether considering public or private aspects of experience, the implication is that to learn is to be shaped by that experience, to have learned something from that experience. When we read a resume, for example, we assume not that the person has simply held a particular job, but that he or she has been shaped in some way, has benefited in some way, from the experience identified. Experience has the characteristic of a resume, in which experience references a particular set of events that have been lived. Experience takes on a currency, a value in the marketplace in the sense that experience itself is linked to knowledge, expertise, and competency (see, for example, Ericsson & Lehmann, 1996). Thus, to consider experience as the basis of learning is to consider also the social context that shapes the experience.

A life is lived as a continuous series of events, but one's individual awareness of the experience represents a break in the continuity of activity. Richard Palmer, a student of the philosopher Hans Gadamer, relied on a rather violent metaphor: He wrote that "in experience, ... there is a shattering of expectations" (1969, p. 232). From the shattered expectations emerges learning: "Since experience contradicts our expectations, [it] is the great teacher for which there is no substitute" (p. 232) in the sense that we learn when "an experience runs counter to our expectations" (Palmer, 1969, p. 196). "It is the 'experienced' man," he noted, "who knows the limitations of all anticipation, the insecurity of all human plans. Yet this does not render him rigid and dogmatic but rather open for new experience.... Experience teaches the incompleteness of all plans" (p. 196).

The emphasis here is on the interaction between a person and the environment (James & Kuklick, 1980). Jack Mezirow (1991) referred to the break in continuity of experience as a disorienting dilemma and believed that a disorienting dilemma arose from life crisis or transition. For Mezirow, the disorienting dilemma led to transformative learning that provided the individual new insights into his or her place in the world. This insight led to emancipation and freedom from constraints, which led to a deeper understanding of the external forces and internal assumptions that held an individual back from realizing his or her full potential. Robert Kegan (1998) offered a similar format for learning, but viewed the transformation process as linear and progressive. Whereas Mezirow emphasized the transformative power of specific events or life experiences, Kegan viewed learning as a slow and steady process in which experiences accumulate, leading to a transformation.

THE CONTRIBUTION OF JOHN DEWEY

John Dewey, one of America's most influential philosophers, introduced the world to a new way of thinking about human learning. Dewey saw experience as an integration of emotions, thoughts, and habits. John Dewey offered one of the first comprehensive descriptions of learning as a holistic process grounded in experience. The late organizational theorist Michael Cohen (2007) expressed Dewey's concept of learning as "the never ending refinement of habits, feelings, and beliefs" (p. 775).

In his various works, including the highly influential book, *Experience and Education*, Dewey contrasted mechanical approaches to learning with learning from experience. He equated mechanical learning with memorizing, pattern matching, and repetition. These types of learning help people learn subjects like math, basic grammar, and other core knowledge. Without these forms of mechanical learning, people would never learn to read or to understand science and technology. Although Dewey understood the importance of mechanical learning, he believed too much emphasis was placed on it. He advocated for a more robust explanation of learning: a learning that helped people move beyond mechanical learning to solve practical problems.

Dewey brought a philosophical clarity to the importance of experience in learning. For Dewey, a philosophy of human behavior was a philosophy of learning. Human beings are above all creatures of learning. Learning for mammals is a process of adaptation that involves responding to the environment. Unlike our counterparts, who respond mainly to stimuli from the external environment, people exercise a great level of control over both their environment and what they choose to learn. Rather than seeing human behavior determined primarily by response to the environment, Dewey focused on reflection experiences. It was experience, rather than our pure adaptation to the environment, that distinguished humans. With this distinction between learning as a purely adaptive process versus learning as an adaptive process of intention and action, we can begin to understand the distinction between experiential learning and mechanical learning.

Dewey (1938) was both a humanist and a pragmatist. He reflected his pragmatic humanism in the question: "To what avail is it to learn something if in the process a person loses his soul?" (p. 49). He was a pragmatist in that he believed learning improved a person's ability to solve problems. Dewey placed a new type of emphasis on learning and built a philosophy of learning based on identifying and solving problems. The approach would become known as pragmatism. Pragmatism grew out of the belief that a philosophy of learning should not simply

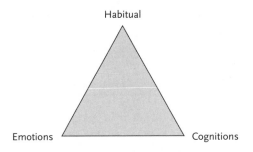

Figure 1.2:
Dewey's underlying structure of experience.

describe the process of learning, but should seek to improve the world by addressing and improving the human condition (Menand, 2001, p. 362).

As a humanist, Dewey stood in contrast to the cognitive philosophers who focused on the mind as the basis of human experience. He was a humanist because he advocated for a learning that was important not only for one's career, but also for developing into one's full potential as a human. As human beings, we hold an awareness of our own ability to learn, and this leads us to develop a greater capacity to learn throughout our lives. Unlike the cognitive philosophers, those who focused on the mind as the basis of human motivation, Dewey focused on how people learn as they reflect on experience. Human experience did not occur in isolated events, but unfolded through a series of interlocking experiences. Learning emerged when individuals reflected on the unfolding and interlocking experiences. Dewey described learning as a largely inductive process in which individual experience serves as the basis of knowledge. This experience must then be analyzed and compared with other forms of knowledge. As an inductive process, learning involves looking closely at the particulars of a situation and then using reasoning to build a more complete understanding of that situation. Each new experience modifies the last experience, so that, over time, individual habits, emotions, and cognitions become an accumulation of life experiences. Thus, we arrive at the core of Dewey's underlying structure of experience: the interplay between emotions, habits, and cognitions, as reflected in Figure 1.2.

COLLATERAL LEARNING

Learning is a process of discovery and insight that emerges when an individual or an organization reflects on its experience. The result is an improved ability to navigate difficult and ambiguous situations. Dewey recognized that learning often emerges as an unintended consequence or outgrowth of the problem-solving process. He called this process—in which certain things are learned even though there was no intention to learn them—"collateral learning" (1938, p. 48). Collateral learning occurs when a person learns something indirectly as a result of another activity. Unintended learning results in attitudes, dislikes or likes, and even the desire to continue learning. It emerges when a person is open to new experiences, learns through exploring, and takes risks. Collateral learning is often just as important as the actual learning goal.

Research evidence supports the idea that certain types of learning activities can lead to unintended but important insights. Miner, Bassoff, and Moorman (2001) found that when organizational members engaged in improvisational learning, collateral insights often transformed into organizational learning. Collateral learning plays an important role in organizations because it points to the importance of context for learning. The concept of collateral learning is related to vicarious learning (see Hoover, Giambatista, & Belkin, 2012; Kim & Miner, 2007), but not perfectly because vicarious learning emerges through goal-directed learning, whereas collateral learning emerges as an indirect process of something collateral to the original goal.

THREE TYPES OF LEARNING EXPERIENCES

Dewey outlined three types of experiences that produce learning: nonlearning experiences, misdirected learning experiences, and learning-directed experiences. Nonlearning experiences describe events in life when we learned nothing. This type is more common in the context of daily decisions and actions in organizations than it is from formal study. Nonlearning experiences occur every day because individuals fall into set routines, fail to reflect on experience, take certain cause-and-effect relationships for granted, and fail to try new things. Jim Robinson, the executive director of the Center for Excellence in Public Leadership at The George Washington University and a lifelong educator, distinguished between experience and learning. "You can repeat the same experience 50 times or you can learn from each experience as if it is a new experience each time," he said. The noneducative experience describes many managers and leaders who go through their work and never learn or change their routine. In nonlearning experiences, actions become automatic.

Misdirected experience describes a second type of experience. The misdirected experience leads to learning the wrong lesson. Since Dewey, the field of psychology has identified a long list of psychological tricks that people play on themselves that lead them to the wrong lesson. Failures of perception, self-assurance, or identity-saving measures keep people from learning from experience. How many times do managers learn the wrong lesson from an experience, only to go on and repeat the same mistake? Experience, at its core, is a reference point. It is why learning in adulthood is different from learning in childhood. An adult has multiple reference points, whereas a child has fewer reference points from which to draw. Unfortunately, too often these reference points can also cloud real learning as an adult seeks to defend an existing interpretation of an event, protect his or her perception and identity, or maintain a public image.

The learning-directed experience represents a third type of experience for which Dewey showed the most enthusiasm. The learning-directed experience holds the power to ignite transformational learning. A learning-directed experience, he wrote, "arouses curiosity, strengthens initiative, and sets up desires and purposes that are sufficiently intense to carry a person over dead places in the future" (1938, p. 38). Learning-directed experiences create opportunities for growth as they create new opportunities for learning. In contrast, nonlearning experiences and misdirected experiences not only fail to be learning experiences, but fail to provide the basis for future learning.

KOLB'S EXPERIENTIAL LEARNING CYCLE

Dewey's philosophy of learning continues to be influential. David Kolb (1984) recognized the value of Dewey's ideas about learning and synthesized them with approaches offered by other learning theorists. Kolb integrated the ideas of psychologist William James, French child psychologist Jean Piaget, Russian psychologist Lev Vygotsky, and organizational theorist Kurt Lewin, among others. His synthesis resulted in a description of learning as a fourfold process, which involves experience, reflection, abstraction, and action.

Kolb's model presents learning along two interrelated dimensions. The first dimension, depicted on the vertical axis, involves knowledge gathering. Knowledge can be gathered from direct experience or abstract concepts. The second dimension, depicted on the horizontal axis, involves knowledge processing. Knowledge can be processed through active experimentation or reflection. Taken together, the two dimensions represent a holistic, multidimensional, and integrated picture of the learning process.

Learning is characterized as a tension-filled process. Learners first must resolve the tension between learning from their direct engagement with the world through experience and the subsequent sensations or emotions that emerge from that experience. When engaging with the world, learners might take a walk or engage in conversation. On the other hand, learners might seek to resolve the tension of learning by seeking abstract ideas or concepts, such as taking a class, reading a book, or listening to music. Learners must also resolve the tension associated with information processing. The information-processing dimension involves two opposing demands. To resolve the tension of knowledge processing, learners must choose between learning from reflection (going inward to analyze a situation) and experimentation (testing the idea in the external environment). For example, learners might keep a journal or spend time observing. When learners engage with another person or test out their ideas, they are resolving the tension of information processing through experimentation.

Kolb's model describes four interrelated learning processes.

- Concrete experience involves active engagement with the world and includes learning through the senses, through direct experience, and through interaction with others. The specific types of knowledge associated with this dimension are sensation, feelings, emotions, and hormonal responses.
- Reflective observation involves organizing thoughts, putting ideas on paper or into models, and observing situations or others.
- Abstract conceptualization involves learning through ideas, concepts, and abstract forms of knowledge. Abstract conceptualization is associated with cognitive processes, codified knowledge like laws, academic research, and institutionalized knowledge such as reports.
- Active experimentation involves taking action on ideas, theories, or plans and focuses on active engagement with the world. Unlike concrete experience, in which the focus is on the emotions generated through interaction, the focus of active experimentation is on the action or behavior.

The fourfold model of learning has been widely accepted for a number of reasons. Kolb's model integrates a variety of learning theories and thus crosses theoretical boundaries. Kolb integrates approaches to learning from the behavioral, cognitive, and social/constructivist approaches into a comprehensive framework for understanding learning. For Kolb, however, learning is more than simply a process associated with formal education or informal learning. Learning is also a process of problem solving and decision making. Because Kolb drew extensively on the experiential learning tradition of John Dewey, the experiential learning model he proposes is built on a valuable philosophical foundation rooted in American pragmatic thinking. Kolb's model of learning continues to attract wide support due to its theoretical coherence and practical value. Even though the model has been subject to criticism on philosophical grounds, it remains arguably the most influential learning theory in a generation.

Kolb's experiential learning model has also gained currency because it offers both a normative and a descriptive model of learning from experience. The model is normative in that it describes an idealized view of learning, but at the same time the model is descriptive in that it provides a description of learning that is consistent with people's experience. The fourfold model provides an actionable series of steps that individuals can take to improve their learning. The model can also be used to solve problems and address situations that are encountered in organizations on a regular basis. As such, Kolb's model builds on Dewey's pragmatic approach and offers a systematic problem-solving and decision-making tool. Simply stated, Kolb's learning cycle has been shown to be a useful tool to improve learning in a variety of circumstances.

A POSTSTRUCTURAL APPROACH TO LEARNING

To say that learning from experience occurs in organizations is to describe a continuous process of learning that emerges from the interaction among emotions, cognitions, and habits. The question arises as to whether learning has an underlying structure, as proposed by Kolb, or whether learning is best conceived as an unstructured process subject to certain environmental and cognitive constraints, but nonetheless without a self-contained arrangement. For example, I (Kayes, 2003) offered that a reinterpretation of experiential learning from a "poststructural approach" opens up new possibilities for understanding Dewey and Kolb not as definitive descriptions of learning, but as guiding interpretive frameworks.

The structure–nonstructure debate is not confined to debates in learning (Kurzweil, 1996). Other inquiries have struggled with the limits and the benefits of structural approaches to learning. A structural approach offers benefits to social science. Structures are more easily measured, offer practical guidance, and enjoy conceptual clarity. Poststructural approaches, what I refer to as "qualitative approaches," offer more detailed and open-ended considerations. Both are essential from a pragmatic point of view.

When experiential learning is embedded in a poststructural context, many of its criticisms (see, for example, Holman, Pavlica, & Thorpe, 1997; Vince, 1998) disappear. A poststructural consideration of learning accepts both the public and private aspects of experience outlined by Scharf. It suggests that although subjective personal experience provides the raw material for learning, experience is always embedded in a context of human pattern, routine, or tradition. This description is reminiscent of the roots of the word: the word "learn" shares the same root as the word "lore," as in folklore. Thus, learning is a way to acquire an understanding of traditions and stories in the context of solving problems or answering pragmatic questions.

A poststructural approach to learning involves processes that roughly track Kolb's learning cycle. *Experience itself* involves an interaction between emotions, thinking, and habits. This interaction instigates the learning process. Experience, although embedded in a social context, is largely psychological because it emerges out of an internal need that both motivates and drives the learning process. The need might be to solve a problem, discover a solution, test a hypothesis, or pursue a goal. The interaction among emotions, habits, and cognitions mirrors Kolb's concrete experience phase of the learning cycle. Second, learning involves an *internal representation* of this experience. The internal representation phase mirrors Kolb's reflective observation phase. Internal representation always relies on *identity*, which is the third aspect of learning. Identity describes how individuals see themselves in the world, their self-narrative, and the stories they tell about themselves. The identify phase tracks Kolb's abstract conceptualization phase because the representation of one's self in the world is always hypothetical, grounded in possibilities and self-perceptions. Finally, the cycle of learning can be complete by integrating *social interaction* (Aten, Nardon, & Steers, 2009).

Note the distinctive phrase used throughout the book: *learning in organizations*. Learning in organizations implies a human activity that occurs in organizations. In contrast, phrases such as "the learning organization" or "organizational learning" emphasize abstractions rather than the human development aspects of learning. A human development approach emphasizes the emotional, cognitive, and habitual patterns that translate into organizational practices, beliefs, identity, and culture.

CONCLUSION

This chapter has outlined some underlying assumptions to guide discussions of learning from experience in organizations. Experience has both a social component and a personal component. During the course of daily events, one becomes aware of experience once the perceived continuity of experience is interrupted. Experience itself consists of three elements—emotions, cognitions, and habits—and becomes transformed into organizational processes. Organizational learning emerges when experience is transformed and becomes embedded in these organizational processes. Much of what constitutes learning in organizations occurs as collateral learning, which is the result of, but not directly related to, a specific learning goal or stated outcome. Thus, although learning is important to improving organizations, much learning does not result directly from planned learning interventions.

CHAPTER 2

The Structure of Learning in Organizations

LEARNING FROM EXPERIENCE IN ORGANIZATIONS

Any consideration of learning in organizations requires a description of how individual learning translates into organizational practice. This description must account for not only the role of experience, but also the mechanisms by which experience translates into organizational learning. Cohen (2007) provided an entry point by calling upon Dewey's description of the interplay between habit, emotion, and cognition and the notion of routine. Highlighting the importance of routine in understanding organizational practices, Cohen defined routines roughly as "reoccurring action patterns" (2007, p. 773) and compared routines with common organizational terms such as practices, collective mind, programs, and standard operating procedures. Four misconceptions are associated with routines, Cohen argued. One misconception is that routines are rigid—following the same pattern without thought. A second misconception is that routines are mundane or not important. A third misconception is that routines are mindless because they are not connected with feelings, reflections, or attention. The fourth misconception is that routines are reflected in recipes because they are often codified, even if this codification exists in one's head. Too often, Cohen claimed, routines are considered uneducative experiences. Thoughtless and emotionless, routines can lead to miseducative or noneducative experiences. At the same time, routines can be informed by emotions and cognition, what he tentatively called "living routines," characterized by flexibility, importance, and thoughtfulness (2007, p. 780). Table 2.1 provides a preliminary list of organizational processes associated with emotions, habits, and cognitions and the interactions between them.

Table 2.1. ORGANIZATIONAL PROCESSES ASSOCIATED WITH
VARIOUS EXPERIENTIAL MODES

Experiential mode	Organizational learning processes
Habit	Efficiency, rote memorization, mechanical learning, routines
Cognition	Task proficiency, analytics, critical thinking, integrative complexity, interpretative processes
Emotion	Self-awareness, anxiety, stress, conflict, emotional contagion
Habit + emotion	Shared values, coherence, culture, climate
Cognition + emotion	Self-awareness, identity, work life, motivation
Cognition + habit	Heedful interrelating, sensemaking
Emotion + cognition + habit	Mindfulness, flow, deliberate practice, adaptability

ROUTINE AND LEARNING

Experience itself is at the center of learning; learning involves the capacity to translate individual experiences into organizational effectiveness through the skills of the organizational member (Stinchcombe, 1990). If the routine allows an individual to exercise a large amount of discretion, then the routine is interactive and depends largely on the individual's skills at performing the task. On the other hand, if the tasks are preformed, then the individual has little control over the routine. Routines are valuable: They make organizations more efficient and productive by capturing innovation and improvements. Without routines, organizations would need to create processes over and over again. On the other hand, routines can also be a problem for organizations because routines may not always be effective and may in fact limit production. Routines also create another problem: Complex knowledge work requires individuals and units to exercise greater discretion over individual tasks. The factors that threaten the effectiveness of routines are variability and uncertainty (Stinchcombe, 1990, p. 22). In order to effectively execute a routine or routines, individual's within the organization rely on knowledge of the system and self-awareness of their own skills. Stinchcombe referred to these elements as principles. Principles were the stuff of individual knowledge that translated into organizational effectiveness through routine. Routine, then, is the central mechanism that translates individual learning into organizational learning.

Routine and novel operational experiences constitute one dimension of learning characterized by two distinct modes of operation (Day & Zaccaro, 2004). How individuals experience the shift from routine to novel and how they learn from each type of experience is essential. Useem, Cook, and Sutton (2005) described the shift from routine to novel experiences that occurred when firefighters encountered new information and began to see that a fire contained greater risk than they had thought just moments before. Interestingly, rather than focus on the cognitive or task-related factors of their experience, Useem and his colleagues focused on the experiences associated with failure. They suggested that certain types of experiences can help prepare individuals to navigate the shift from routine to novelty. Learning is the key to navigating this shift. As failure emerges, the need for learning becomes more pronounced and the absence of learning during failure only further fuels the crisis. When the switch from routine to novel occurs, the demands can quickly exceed the individual's capacity to learn (Kegan, 1998).

SHIFTING FROM ROUTINE TO NOVEL

One key distinguishing factor associated with the shift from routine to novel is the expectation of the shift itself. During routine activity, the environmental demands conform to expectations. Novel situations, on the other hand, fail to conform to expectations (see Lewis & Dehler, 2000). Table 2.2 outlines the learning challenges associated with shifting from routine to novel learning situations. Responding to the shift from routine to novel requires the acquisition of skills to deal with heightened levels of anxiety (Vince, 1998; see also Stein, 2004). Novel experiences are defined by their lack of apparent task constraints and therefore are less likely to be solved by typical expertise. Novel experiences

Table 2.2. LEARNING CHALLENGES ASSOCIATED WITH SHIFTING FROM ROUTINE TO NOVEL LEARNING SITUATIONS

Aspects of experience	Routine learning	Knowledge transformation	Novel learning
Cognitive	My model of the system matches situation complexity	Change mental models	Adaptive mental models
Emotional	Emotions initiate and sustain learning	Master stress, anxiety, conflict	Emotional self-control under stress, recognition, and response to anxiety
Habitual	Behaviors accomplish goals	Change behaviors, develop new skills and habits	Skilled at adaptability and change
Culture	Values facilitate goal achievement and harness learning	Change values	Valuing of learning and psychological safety
Identity	I see myself as competent at this task	Change self-concept, flexible	Multiple identities, contextual, and interdependent
Collective commitment	We agree on goals, direction, and vision	Change goals, direction, or vision	Multiple and shifting goals

		Evidence	Counter experience
	High	Routine, proven, high consensus on evidence; builds basic beliefs about cause and effect relationships through data and interpretation	Challenge routine, experiment, invent environment, learn by doing
Consensus on evidence			
	Low	Direct experience Prior knowledge, precedent, unverified knowledge; builds basic belief about cause and effect relationships through direct observation and interpretation	Exploration Coordinate, engage in trial and error, search for new forms or explanations of causal probability
		Routine	Novel
		Operational context	

Figure 2.1:
Types of learning from experience.

also share characteristics with ill-structured problems because the goal to be achieved is not clear, and the path to solving the problem is not clear (e.g., King & Kitchener, 1994).

A second dimension comes into play in learning in organizations: the degree of consensus within organizations. Consensus helps us understand the degree to which experience can be considered an organizational phenomenon (Scott, 1995). Fiol (1994) argued that consensus around knowledge provides the opportunity for taking action on knowledge and that organizations may form consensus on certain aspects of meaning and not others. Thus, consensus around meaning provides the foundation for learning and collective action taking (Nelson & Winters, 1982). A framework of learning from experience in organizations is based on two dimensions. The first dimension considers the degree of consensus that has emerged around the nature of the knowledge. The second dimension considers whether the situation is routine or novel. Figure 2.1 illustrates four distinct types of learning from experience associated with the combination of the two dimensions of experience: routine or novelty and the degree of consensus achieved within an organization.

LEARNING FROM DIRECT EXPERIENCE

One form of learning is learning from direct experience. This is what we commonly think of when we think about learning from experience. Learning from direct experience is consistent with Kolb's initial formulation of learning. It describes how managers draw on past experience to assess, reflect upon, and revise their view of cause-and-effect relationships. Experiential learning often results in developing new insights, revising actions, and fostering new experiences that lead to greater learning in light of analysis of this experience (Kolb, 1984). Experience emerges from a break in perception of continuity. Richard Palmer, a student of the philosopher Hans Gadamer, characterized experience as "a shattering of expectations" (p. 232). From the shattered expectations emerges learning.

LEARNING FROM COUNTER EXPERIENCE

In the introduction to their collected readings on counterfactual thinking, Mandel, Hilton, and Catellani (2005) described our amazing ability to recollect experiences from our past in order to shape a coherent identity. Even more amazing, they believed, is our ability to relive or rethink these events as if they happened differently. Learning from experience is not always a factor of what did happen in a historical sense; it also involves imagining a different outcome.

Counter experiential learning—also known as counterfactual learning or the psychology of "what if"—uses events that have never happened or nearly happened as the substance of learning. Learning from counter experience is required when an organization doesn't have the luxury of repeating an experience. The outcome of counter experiential learning is the development of insights from certain kinds of experiences that are either low probability or of such consequences that having the experience would be catastrophic.

Morris and Moore (2000) argued that some kinds of evidence actually serve as a barrier to learning. When faced with certain types of evidence, managers tend to downplay internal reflection and instead focus on external causes ("others") or worse alternatives (downward comparison). Counter experiences allow individuals to draw lessons to improve performance. In particular, drawing lessons that are both upward, expressing the possibility of improving performance, and directed at self are likely to improve performance. In other words, counter experiences seem to be of particular value when the content of the analysis is aimed at improving performance rather than trying to avoid poor performance and is focused on what the individual conducting the analysis could do in the situation rather than looking at what others should do. The best lessons learned from counter experience, then, are lessons focused on how the individual can improve his or her performance.

LEARNING FROM EVIDENCE

The fourth type of learning from experience involves learning from the indirect experiences of others. When learning from evidence occurs, learning does not emanate from direct experience, but from the accumulated experiences of others, captured systematically and interpreted within the context of current problems. Learning from indirect experience, like learning from evidence, occurs as individuals learn from the experiences, research, or ideas of others. Learning from indirect experience is the primary source of learning for most formalized training programs, including traditional education. Learning from indirect experiences is the primary goal of evidence-based learning.

There is growing interest in an evidence-based learning approach within the field of organizations and management (Briner, Denyer, & Rousseau, 2009; Graen, 2009; Pfeffer & Sutton, 2006; Rousseau & McCarthy, 2007). Evidence-based management involves making managerial decisions based on the best available scientific evidence. Pfeffer and Sutton commented that evidence-based management involves "using better, deeper logic and employing facts to the extent possible" and "permits leaders to do their jobs better" (2006, p. 13). Calls for evidence-based approaches to management often reference the success of evidence management in high-consensus fields like finance, medicine, and education. The field of evidence-based management seeks to make scholarly research applicable to practice, to gain influence as a field, and to encourage practicing managers to draw from research to guide action. For example, Pfeffer and Sutton cited evidence from an experimental study to note a rather interesting application of evidence-based management (Bluedorn, Turban, & Love, 1999). They argued that a company like Chevron could save more than 6,000 hours in unproductive meetings each year simply by having employees stand up during meetings. Evidence from the study showed that standing rather than sitting produces meetings that are 34% shorter but have equal quality in decision making.

LEARNING FROM EXPLORATION

Exploratory learning, such as trial and error, describes an attempt to reconfigure cause-and-effect relationships. We can contrast exploratory learning with Morris and Moore's observation that under some circumstances, learning occurs through factors of counterfactual thinking. Based on Morris and Moore's observations, we can propose that counterfactual learning is most appropriate when consensus on the evidence is high and the environment is highly complex. Under these conditions, counterfactual thinking challenges the consensus view but identifies factors that have a low probability of causality. In other words, counterfactual thinking improves decision making in situations when the evidence is solid but causal links are unclear.

Exploratory learning has connections to a stream of learning research (Schulz & Bonawitz, 2007; Schulz, Goodman, Tenebaum, & Jenkins, 2008; see also Kayes & Kayes, 2011, for a discussion) focused on how children use evidence to learn about their environment. Schulz found that subjects are remarkably adaptive when it comes to learning abstract principles of cause and effect. Only a few trials are needed for subjects to develop a reliable model of cause and effect. Interestingly, Schulz found that these mental models, although acquired quickly, are difficult to break once the cause-and-effect patterns no longer hold. Even though Schulz conducted these studies with children, the results suggest patterns for adults too. Managers may hold onto existing beliefs (in the form of cause-and-effect relationships) even after they experience evidence to the contrary. What the researchers found next is telling. When subjects were confronted with data that contradicted existing beliefs, they were more likely to move into a state of exploration and learning to explain the discrepancy. Thus, learning occurred, but only prompted by disconfirming evidence. It seems that exploratory learning resulted when pre-existing experience was challenged by disconfirming cause-and-effect relationships.

ORGANIZATIONAL LEARNING STYLES

Organizations, by their nature, involve unique functions and take on unique forms (Mintzberg, 1979). Kodak led its industry and invested in the first process for capturing digital images, but was unable to realize the commercial value of this technology. Bureaucratic infighting, fear of new products, and an inability to foresee future business scenarios all played a part in Kodak's demise. Despite its history of innovation and new product development, Kodak suffered from its own inability to transform an innovation into a commercially viable product. The most important lesson to learn from Kodak's demise? It failed to learn as an organization. Kodak's business model broke down because it had built its business on one way of learning and was unable to adjust to a new business environment. Said another way, Kodak was a victim of its own organizational learning style.

Learning in organizations follows unique patterns based on the organization's core purpose. Organizations organize learning in four distinct but related ways. Experiential learning theory has already shed light on different forms of organizational learning. In this section I provide a typology to guide leaders in organizations on how to think with more perspicuity about learning in organizations as a multifaceted process.

Different organizations excel at different types of learning. Organizational learning styles emerge as organizations develop unique preferences for how they gather, process, and act upon knowledge (see Ribbens, 1997). Consistent with Dewey, these styles are organizational habits, which reflect both how organizational members learn and more importantly how habits get in the way of learning. Based on Easterby-Smith's (1997) classification of organizational learning, the approach espoused here is consistent with the human development and psychology approach, which emphasizes integration of emotions, cognitions, and behaviors that ultimately lead to a change in values and routines. The ultimate goal of this approach involves "broadening individual repertoires of experiences, skills, and know-how" (p. 1088). An experiential approach emphasizes changing values related to culture and self-concepts related to identity.

Over time, organizations develop unique approaches to learning. These approaches can be organized into four basic processes, in which each process is associated with a corresponding phase of the learning cycle (see Dixon, 1999). Miller (1996) also realized the importance of developing an organizational typology of learning, but he focused on the more macro forces of organizational change and identity rather than the experiential basis of learning. Elkjaer (2001) offered the idea that an experiential learning approach to organizational learning centers on employees' active involvement in the process. Taking Elkjaer's approach to organizational learning a step further, we can imagine that experiences can become organized around various activities. Dewey's concept of *embeddedness* and collateral learning become important. Learning occurs as embeddedness. To understand how people learn from experience, you must first understand the structure embedded within the organization—its symbols, identity, and history and how these elements shape the organization. Unlike the sociological view, however, that sees these symbols as externalities or social norms, the concept of embeddedness suggests that these elements are preserved in human experience. Without understanding how human experience shapes the organization, it is difficult to understand how organizations are shaped by human experience.

The belief that organizations learn in distinct ways may have originated with March's (2011) evolutionary approach to learning. Lawrence and Lorsch (1967) also recognized that the "cognitive and emotional orientations" of managers serve as drivers for organizational differentiation (cited in Kolb, 1984). Differences in cognitive and emotional orientation provide ways to conceptualize distinctions in how organizations learn. Factors other than manager orientation may also impact the organization's learning style. The industry, stakeholder demands, culture, history, and other factors all influence organizational routines. Over time these routines become embedded in the organization and influence how it learns, and organizations become adept at functioning in parts of the learning process. These knowledge processing routines become associated with the organizational learning style.

Organizational learning styles describe four types of organizations based on their primary learning function: knowledge generation, analysis, innovation, and application.

Knowledge Generation

The knowledge-generating organization is concerned with generating new ideas, new knowledge, and innovation. The emphasis is on novelty, and the organization is less concerned with accuracy, practicality, or applicability. The knowledge-generating function of learning in organizations focuses on keeping the organization up to date so that it can both explore new possibilities and adapt to changes in the environment. Contemporary news organizations serve as an archetype of this kind of organization.

Knowledge Analysis

The knowledge-analyzing organization is concerned primarily with developing a comprehensive understanding of a problem and creating coherent, well-designed plans for the future. The knowledge-analyzing organization focuses on abstract theories and concepts and attempts to generate new ways of understanding. Like the knowledge-generating organization, the knowledge-analyzing organization recognizes the value of dealing with increasing amounts of information. Where the knowledge-generating organization is intent on producing increasing amounts of information, the knowledge-analyzing organization is intent on interpreting increasing amounts of information. In the knowledge-analyzing organization, the organization does not necessarily seek to find a practical use for knowledge; that is the primary function of the knowledge-innovating organization.

Knowledge Innovation

The knowledge-innovating organization focuses on putting new ideas, inventions, and thinking into action. It is within the knowledge-innovating organization that organizational activity is directed at solving and revolutionizing practical issues. An example of an organization that primarily focuses on knowledge innovation is a venture capital–funded startup.

Knowledge Application

The knowledge application and improvement organization focuses on improving existing processes, knowledge, and ideas. Learning emerges, but it is not innovative or breakthrough learning; rather, this type of learning is incremental and helps the organization improve basic functions by becoming better, more productive, or more adept at activities it already does. Table 2.3 summarizes key organizational learning processes associated with each organizational learning style.

Table 2.3. TYPES, PURPOSES, FUNCTIONS, AND ARCHETYPES
OF ORGANIZATIONAL LEARNING

Type	Purpose	Archetype
Knowledge generating	Concerned with generating new ideas, knowledge, and information. Primary objective is new information; less concerned with practicality or accuracy.	The contemporary news organization. Knowledge for the sake of uniqueness and originality.
Knowledge analyzing	Concerned with developing comprehensive understanding, new theories, or ideas.	The research university. Knowledge for the sake of understanding.
Knowledge innovating	Concerned with putting ideas into practice, generating ideas that can solve problems or provide new ways of getting things done.	Venture capital–funded startup. Knowledge for the sake of solving a new problem or creating something new.
Knowledge operating	Concerned with how knowledge can improve performance, be put to practice to generate income, or take action.	Hedge funds. Knowledge for the sake of making a profit.

CONCLUSION

This chapter has outlined considerations for how learning from experience translates into organizational processes and functions. Learning from experience can occur along four distinct but interconnected dimensions based on the nature of the knowledge learned and the operational context. These processes can be translated into four unique organizational "learning styles" that describe patterns of interaction within an organization that help the organization learn. These learning styles identify specific modes associated with how organizations gather, process, and act upon knowledge. These patterns offer unique learning preferences for organizations but can result in organizational rigidity, and it is often difficult to transition between different learning modes. These learning preferences provide insight into how organizational failure occurs.

CHAPTER 3
Learning versus Performance in the Air France Flight 447 Disaster

THE BREAKDOWN OF AIR FRANCE FLIGHT 447

In the cockpit of the Airbus 330 sat two co-pilots, David Robert, aged 37, and Pierre Bonin, aged 32. The flight captain, Marc Dubois, aged 58, headed back into the cabin for a break. Over the Atlantic Ocean, nearly 400 miles off the coast of Brazil, the Airbus 330 encountered a concerning but not unique weather pattern. The in-flight radar revealed a small storm, and Robert and Bonin decided to improve in-flight conditions by ascending to a higher altitude and reducing air speed. What the pilots could not see from their radar was that behind the small storm sat another weather system, perhaps 10 times larger than the one they observed (Scott, 2010). At this point in the flight, the crew flew out of communication with air traffic control in Brazil, where they had just departed, and Paris, their destination. Earlier in the flight, they had expressed concern that they were not able to locate the coordinates of a predesignated runway that could be used for emergency purposes, although they had no reason to suspect that they would need it.

The crew confidently commanded an Airbus 330, known as an A330. The pilots had reason to remain confident in their equipment. The transcripts from the cockpit flight data recorder, which was recovered at the accident site, revealed their confidence. As they slowly guided the aircraft to higher altitude, Bonin remarked, "Lucky we're on a 330, eh? We wouldn't be so clever if we were on a full 340" (BEA, 2012, p. 21), referring to the Airbus 340. In contrast to the A330, which they commanded, the A340, which had additional engines, was known to be more difficult to fly at higher altitude. There are nearly 700 A330s in operation, and the pilots likely knew that the model had never been involved in a fatal accident.

The aircraft was equipped with the latest computer technology, the most sophisticated censors, and advanced computer software. Its "fly-by-wire" technology eliminated the need for hydraulic controls. Because of the aircraft's advanced systems, pilots needed to understand how to operate it in distinct operational modes. For example, in "auto mode," the onboard computer set parameters for the flight. When the pilot executed a new command, the pilot's input was then reviewed by the computer, which in turn determined if the command fit into predefined parameters and only then executed the command. This complicated process took only milliseconds, assuming the pilot's command fit these predefined parameters. When flying in "auto mode," the pilot acted within a very narrow set of flight operation procedures. The onboard flight computer reviewed every input made by a pilot, including altitude changes, flight speed corrections, and rudder changes. In contrast to auto mode, "manual mode" required the pilot crew to set the parameters and put the crew in direct control of the aircraft.

The cockpit of an A330 is a shrine to the possibilities of modern technology. The in-flight instruments have computer-generated images, creating the illusion of a computer simulation. In the A330, a mechanical joystick replaces the steering wheel typically associated with flying a plane. The joystick creates simplicity in operation, like the controller on a home video game. The joystick sits to the outside of the pilots, not in the center, so one pilot cannot directly see the position of the joystick controlled by the other pilot.

In addition to electronic flight controls, fly-by-wire mechanics, and various operational modes, the A330 is equipped with the Aircraft Communications Addressing and Reporting System, or ACARS. The onboard ACARS transmits repair and maintenance reports directly to a maintenance center in Paris through satellite communication. On Air France Flight 447 (AF 447), the ACARS issued 24 reports in the last 4 minutes of the flight, but this information was not available to the crew inside the cockpit of the A330.

Soon after it entered the storm, the sound of ice crystals forming on the outside of the aircraft could be heard in the cockpit. Less than a minute later, the autopilot disconnect warning signal was generated by the onboard computer (BEA, 2012, p. 23). Robert took control of the aircraft and the warning signal stopped. About a minute later, a stall warning sounded. The crew reviewed the airspeed indicators in the cockpit, but the various gauges showed inconsistent information. In order to stay in the sky and maintain lift, an A330 must maintain an airspeed of nearly 500 miles an hour. Anything slower results in a stall, a dangerous situation in which an aircraft loses lift, the very act of nature that allows it to fly. Bonin and Robert shared their observation with one another:

"We haven't got a good display," Bonin said.
"We've lost [air speed]," Robert added.

The less experienced of the two pilots, 32-year-old Bonin, took control of the plane as the two pilots struggled to gain a grasp of the situation. Bonin pulled the joystick back, which caused the aircraft to pitch upward. This shifted the plane from a horizontal position to a position with the nose up (BEA, 2012, p. 9). The aircraft was already flying at a reasonably high altitude to avoid the worst of the storm. Ascending any higher—exactly what would happen by pointing the nose up—took the plane dangerously close to its flying "envelope," its maximum safe flying altitude.

The crew then called for the captain, but the captain failed to respond. By the time the captain returned to the cockpit, the A330 and the cockpit crew expressed only confusion over the actual airspeed, altitude, and pitch of the plane. It appeared the crew no longer trusted the instruments.

"What's happening? I don't know, I don't know what's happening," reported Robert.
"We're losing control of the aero plane there," Bonin stated.
"We lost all control of the aero plane, we don't understand anything, we've tried everything," responded Robert.

BEA, 2012, p. 27

The captain, now sitting behind the two pilots, also expressed confusion as he attempted to unravel the plane's condition. Only at this point did Robert learn that Bonin had been pulling back on the joystick; Robert knew that such an action in their situation would cause the plane to lose altitude. Robert then engaged Bonin about the direction of the joystick:

"But I've been at maxi nose-up for a while!" shouted Bonin.
"No, no, no … don't climb," responded Robert. "So go down…. Give me the controls…. Give me the controls!"

BEA, 2012, p. 31

About 6 minutes after the first warning signal sounded, AF 447 crashed into the Atlantic Ocean, about 450 miles off the coast of Brazil. The black box data recorder, recovered from the scene, revealed that the aircraft maintained an air-speed of 120 miles an hour at the time of impact (Wise, 2011).

FACTORS THAT COMPLICATE LEARNING

The Air France disaster is tragic. It perplexed investigators because it didn't follow typical patterns of organizational disaster. As James Reason (1990) explained, most accidents can be traced to a chain of events that, had any one event been avoided, the accident itself would likely have been avoided. The AF 447 disaster didn't follow this time-tested pattern. Rather than a chain of events, the disaster resulted from the inability to respond to a situation. The pilots commanding the AF 447 experienced a shift from routine to novel and this shift highlights why it is important to understand the connection between learning and resilience: The ability of the crew to recover the aircraft required a qualitative shift in how they learned.

Of particular interest is how the subcrew of Bonin and Robert responded to the initial equipment failure. Rather than pitching the nose of the aircraft, as Bonin did, experts indicate that adjusting the engine to 85% thrust and leveling the nose with five degrees of pitch should have recovered the aircraft (see Ross & Tweedie, 2012; Wise, 2012). If the first action should have been to level the aircraft, then why did Bonin pull back on the stick? By pulling back on the joystick, he unknowingly ensured that the aircraft continued to lose altitude and airspeed. Even after the computer re-engaged and the aircraft was back in auto mode, Bonin continued to put the aircraft in a more severe pitch by pulling back on the joystick and causing the aircraft to descend at an alarming rate.

Poorly Developed Team

One factor that complicated learning and may have contributed to Bonin's decision to pull back on the joystick was a poorly developed team. Captain Dubois and his team of pilots, Robert and Bonin, may have had the deck stacked against them from the moment they entered the cockpit. The disadvantage came because they found themselves part of an ad hoc team (Sundstrom, DeMeuse, & Futrell, 1990). In an ad hoc team, the team members come together for a short time, complete an activity, and then quickly disband. Ad hoc teams commonly perform, produce, or manage projects. This is why they are also referred to as project teams. Ad hoc teams lack continuity in membership, norms, and tasks and, therefore, often fail to build the underlying patterns of behavior that support learning.

Ad hoc teams find it difficult to learn because team members have spent less time developing interpersonal dynamics and, thus, members remain unfamiliar with each other. Members of ad hoc teams tend to hold only a shallow understanding of other team members and their skills, abilities, and how they might react under stress. Void of strong emotional connections between individuals, ad hoc teams require substantive interpersonal development when the group is forming.

Another reason that learning is often difficult in ad hoc teams is because ad hoc teams often lack clear team norms. In many teams, especially newly formed ones, team members lack a clear understanding of what constitutes appropriate behavior in the team. Said another way, team members have not built a shared understanding about acceptable standards of behavior (Feldman, 1994). Teams that fail to define appropriate behavior often fail to review operating procedures, fail to openly address tough questions, and fail to discuss tough issues because these discussions might cause uncomfortable conflict (e.g., Edmondson, 1999). Taking actions such as these would be more likely to generate conflict than to encourage learning in ad hoc teams. Since learning is more likely to occur when social forces such as interpersonal safety, trust, and understanding are present, learning in ad hoc teams is under constant threat. Even more critical, ad hoc team members don't know how individuals will react when the environment requires different forms of learning—say, when a cockpit crew is required to operate in auto mode versus manual mode.

Lack of Clear Leadership

Another reason that ad hoc teams like the one that flew AF 447 have trouble learning is that they are held together by frail leadership which may lead to less than optimal learning as team's become confronted with novel problems (Kayes & Kayes, 2004). When Captain Dubois exited the cockpit for a break, further ambiguity and anxiety emerged between the two remaining pilots, Robert and Bonin. Despite the differences in experience and age between the two remaining crew members, the relationship between them was anything but clear. Without a clear leadership structure, Robert and Bonin were left to negotiate who was now in charge of flying the aircraft. This negotiation takes time. In addition, the pilots would be required to apply teamwork skills, but it is unlikely they were ever trained to display these skills.

When the captain finally returned to the cockpit, the aircraft had lost significant altitude, and he entered a situation in which learning had regressed to the point that the crew was unable to learn what to do in time to save the aircraft from disaster.

Limited Experience

The initial decision by the cockpit crew to ascend to higher altitude was informed by their goal to limit turbulence brought about by flying through the storm. Under most circumstances, this would not have caused any problems, but the wet and cold conditions outside the aircraft caused airspeed sensors to fail. These sensors are located outside the aircraft, just below but out of sight of the cockpit. These small L-shaped sensors are called "pitot tubes." Airbus had issued a warning that explained the pitot tube failures. Airbus had also planned to replace specific models of the tube that might fail under wet and cold conditions, but the company had not yet replaced the pitots on the AF 447 aircraft. Although the pitot failure on AF 447 was reported through ACARS to the Air France maintenance facility in Paris, the failure was not reported directly to the pilots in the cockpit. The accident report issued by BEA, the French air authority, concluded that the pitot tubes led to a faulty airspeed indication in the cockpit. It is not clear if Bonin or Robert knew about the potential for faulty pitots and thus the faulty airspeed indicators, which may explain why they were confused by the airspeed indicators in the cockpit.

Something important happened after the airspeed indicators thawed and began reporting the correct airspeed. The pilots made a full recovery as correct airspeed information was restored. From the standpoint of safely flying the aircraft, the worst was over. But even though the pitot tubes were reporting the correct airspeed and Bonin eased up on the pressure, Bonin continued to push the nose of the plane upward, which at high altitude has the effect of further decreasing airspeed, which in turn re-engages the stall warning yet again. Over the course of the next few minutes, the stall warning sounded 75 times. As Bonin commanded the plane, the computer warned the crew that they had breached the parameters of auto mode. By pointing the nose up, Bonin was doing the exact opposite of what he should have done: Simply adjust the engine to 85% thrust and point the nose up by five degrees to maintain aircraft lift (see Ross & Tweedie, 2012).

The faulty airspeed indicator and confusing messages from an onboard flight system overwhelmed the inexperienced cockpit crew. More experienced crews may not have been so overwhelmed. For example, the PBS show *Nova* (Scott, 2010) conducted an experiment in which two experienced pilots were asked to undergo a simulation. The pilots had not been informed about the nature of the situation they would face. In the simulation, the pilots were presented events similar to those experienced by the pilots on AF 447. Error messages repeatedly sounded throughout the cockpit. The experienced pilots in this simulation seemed to ignore the battery of stall warnings. Once the simulator shifted to manual mode, the experienced pilots appeared to turn their attention away from the computer system. Auto-mode warnings now became only distractions. The pilots set the aircraft engine to 85% thrust and pointed the nose up by five degrees.

The experienced crew seemed to discount the barrage of signals coming from the aircraft and took control of the plane by focusing on a few key variables, namely establishing a safe flight speed and an appropriate pitch to the plane. The experienced crew ignored the computer system and took direct control of the plane. By making a few small adjustments to pitch, engine thrust, and wing position, the pilots flew the plane without having key information about flight parameters. Experience flying a plane, it seems, made a difference in how pilots acted in the face of change.

Bill Voss (2012), head of the Flight Safety Foundation, an organization committed to improving flight safety, provided an explanation for the crash of AF 447 that hinged on the importance of experience and learning. He believed the problems in the cockpit of AF 447 began when the mechanical failure shifted the plane from auto to manual mode. He believed the AF 447 pilots had never experienced such a dramatic shift during flight, nor had they experienced the shift in their training. They became confused by the messages coming from the onboard computer. Their confusion remained until the end.

In order to make the shift from auto to manual operation in these conditions, experience becomes crucial. It is possible, according to Voss, that neither Robert nor Bonin had encountered an in-flight stall at high altitude, nor had the pilots ever trained for such a situation. High-altitude stalls occur infrequently and thus aren't part of pilots' repertoire of experiences, their background knowledge. Further, because the situation is uncommon, training on how to recover from a high-altitude stall is not part of a systematic training program. In planes such as the A330, in which an onboard computer sets parameters, the cockpit crew no longer serves to fly the plane but serves as a backup to the computer.

A partial answer to one of the most troubling questions of the disaster begins to emerge: Why did Bonin continue to pull back on the joystick? The relatively inexperienced Bonin may not have received training in how to recover from a stall at high altitude. The physics of flying in the thin air of 35,000 feet demand different requirements than flying at 10,000 feet. In effect, Bonin was applying a set of criteria that applied at lower altitudes but not higher altitudes. In fact, when Bonin transferred control of the aircraft to Robert, he muttered, "Go ahead, you have the controls. We are still in TOGO eh." TOGO, short for "touch and go," refers to a process of regaining lift at low altitude, something that occurs when a pilot suddenly abandons a landing and reinitiates ascent of the aircraft at the last possible moment. Bonin, it appeared, pulled back on the joystick because he was attempting to execute a recovery from an in-flight stall at low altitude, a process that differs substantially from recovering from a stall at high altitude.

Experience in recovering from a high-altitude in-flight stall wasn't part of a pilot's repertoire of habits, something that the pilots could learn from working under routine conditions. Knowledge and skill in how to recover from a high-altitude in-flight stall could have been learned from direct experience, professional programs, training, or even working with or talking to more experienced others. These were the repertoire of experiences needed by the AF 447 crew.

FROM NORMAL TO ALTERNATE LAW: A SHIFT FROM PERFORMANCE TO LEARNING

Lack of a repertoire in recovering from a high-altitude stall set the stage for disaster—but experience is not destiny, either for the crew of AF 447 or for others who find themselves in a situation for which they have no prior direct experience. People learn from experience, even when they have no direct experience with a particular situation. Problems can be solved, failures responded to, and mishaps corrected even when people lack a repertoire of direct experience. Counter experience, evidence-based learning, and exploration all provide alternatives to learning from direct experience.

A poorly developed team, ambiguous leadership, and lack of experience operating under certain conditions are a few of the factors leading to the breakdown of learning in AF 447. Organizations become vulnerable to breakdown if they fail to learn and adapt in response to shifts in the environment. Shifts in operational demands occur on a regular basis. The shifts could require learning the kinds of information needed, the social dynamics involved, or operational know-how. One type of shift that may have been needed in AF 447 is the shift from performance orientation to a learning orientation, because this change requires a qualitative shift in operational orientation.

The temptation is to consider learning as separate from operations—as preparation for operations. Learning is often relegated to processes that occur before operations, in cases such as training or credentialing. In other cases, learning is relegated to processes that occur after operations, such as after-action reviews or lessons-learned exercises. A more sophisticated consideration of learning understands that learning is a process that also occurs during operations. Learning is not tangential to operations, but is a key to effective operations. In the case of AF 447, learning became essential for the crew to operate the aircraft when it shifted from autopilot to manual operational mode. A better understanding of the design of the A330 helps illustrate the critical nature of this shift.

The A330 is designed to operate in several distinct modes. Two of the most common modes are "normal law" and "alternate law." Under normal conditions, the A330 operates under normal law, what most lay observers would refer to as autopilot. According to the Airbus flight manual, an A330 shifts from normal law to alternate law only after multiple failures occur while operating under normal law (see www.airbusdriver.net, 2012). Under normal law, the crew exercises less control over the aircraft's functioning. For example, it would have been nearly impossible for the crew to stall the A330 while operating under normal law, because the onboard computer system would override crew inputs that might lead to a stall. The same level of oversight does not ensue when the crew operates under alternate law.

Operating under alternate law requires a distinct set of knowledge, skills, and abilities compared with operating under normal law. While operating under normal law, for example, fewer parameters exist. Boundaries of acceptable flight are pre-established, rules of operation are more clearly defined, and cognitive and emotional engagement is minimized. The need for coordination among the members of the crew is minimized because the aircraft mediates the controls. Normal law also limits the need for clear leadership because the onboard computer serves as a kind of proxy for leadership. The burden of operation is placed on the machine itself under normal law.

While operating under alternate law, however, the crew faces a different set of learning demands. Not only must the crew working under alternate law understand the parameters for operation, but the crew must establish the parameters of operation by factoring in the particulars of the situation. While operating under normal law, the AF 447 crew likely focused on the unusual weather pattern, the stall warning, airspeed, and pitch. When the A330 onboard computer shifted to alternate law, something significant happened, not just in flight operation, but also in the demands placed on the pilots.

Team development, leadership, and experience were of little consequence operating under normal law, but they took on new relevance when operating under alternate law. The poorly developed team and lack of clear leadership contributed to the confusion as the crew struggled to fly the aircraft. The crew struggled to explain the stream of error messages emanating from the computer and became distracted from the most important issue they faced: maintaining air speed and lift.

In AF 447, the crew failed to comprehend the situation and failed to coordinate their actions. When the crew noticed a problem with the air speed indicator, their routine quickly required a shift from a performance orientation to a learning orientation. Once the pitot began working, the crisis should have been over and the team should have returned to its routine flight. Instead, the already anxiety-stricken Bonin continued to pull back on the stick. Robert, not clear in his role, failed to comprehend the situation, openly assess the situation, or coordinate with Bonin on correct action. Since shifting into alternate law, Robert remained unaware that Bonin was pulling back on the joystick and was unaware that the aircraft was continuing to lose airspeed because of Bonin's action. The flight data recorder recovered at the accident site showed that just moments after the A330 shifted into alternate law, Robert pushed forward on his joystick, but his efforts only had a moderating effect because the aircraft automatically averaged out the angle of the nose as Bonin continued to push backward.

PERFORMANCE VERSUS LEARNING ROUTINES

As "reoccurring patterns of action," routines often consist of following rigid patterns, reflecting the mundane nature of organizational life. Too often, routine results in actions that are thoughtless, emotionless, and ultimately devoid of learning (Cohen, 2007). Cohen offered that in many cases, while operating under routine conditions, learning never occurs because people are "disengaged" from their world. On the other hand, individuals can engage by infusing their routines with high levels of reflection and being more mindful of their emotions and thoughts. He referred to the situation as "living routines." The distinction between living routines and disengaged routines is captured in the distinction between performance orientation and learning orientation. The performance/learning orientation distinction has appeared in the learning literature for some time (Smiley & Dweck, 1994), but has more recently been adopted in the study of organizations (Kayes, 2009; Seijts, Latham, Tasa, & Latham, 2004; Sitkin, See, Miller, Lawless, & Carton, 2011). Table 3.1 outlines the distinctions between learning and performance among different research traditions.

Performance and learning are distinct orientations. They describe differences in how individuals within organizations approach operations. A learning orientation involves identifying new strategies to solve a problem, being open to new experiences, and actively seeking new opportunities to learn. While individuals who display a strong learning orientation often experience high levels of emotional engagement, their emotions are more stable and balanced. Short-term failures are experienced as temporary setbacks because individuals are confident that they can recover from failure and be successful in the long term as they gain mastery over a task. In contrast, a performance orientation involves focusing on a few variables that are essential to success, demonstrating competence, and seeking success in well-established, measurable, and achievable tasks. Individuals

Table 3.1. CHARACTERISTICS OF LEARNING AND
PERFORMANCE ORIENTATIONS

Area of study	Learning	Performance
Strategy (Sitkin, See, Miller, Lawless, & Carton, 2011)	• Heedfulness/mindfulness • Openness to new experience • Trial and error • Search for new resources and discontinuous advances	• Focus on controllable factors • Initiative to improve • Resistance to negative feedback • Effort and persistence
Team dynamics and goal setting (Kayes, 2006)	• Generation of new strategies for problem solving • Multiple goals • Established work processes • High reliance on new strategies	• Improvement of old strategies for problem solving • Single measurable goals • Difficult-to-maintain processes • High reliance on old strategies
Goal setting and performance (Seijts, Latham, Tasa, & Latham, 2004)	• Generation of new strategies for achieving a goal • Discovery and implementation of task-related strategies	• Achievement of a specific measurable outcome • Effective task performance
Child development (Smiley & Dweck, 1994)	• Concern for mastery of a task • Acceptance of failure • Active challenge-seeking behaviors	• Concern for demonstrating competence and limiting the appearance of incompetence • Preference for problems that are easily doable, avoiding challenges • Cautious avoidance
Adult development (Kegan, 1998)	• "Self-authoring" • Determining one's own destiny • Self-awareness and emotional self-control • Understanding the impact of others on self • Self-determined parameters of success	• Belief that outcomes are out of our control • Reliance on existing rules and procedures • Externally determined parameters of success

who demonstrate a performance orientation display more caution and focus on utilizing past strategies that have proved successful.

One study in particular illustrates why the distinction between a learning and performance orientation is relevant for understanding organizational breakdown. Researchers (Smiley & Dweck, 1994) found that children with a learning orientation showed higher levels of confidence and improved self-evaluation. Children with a learning goal orientation showed lower preoccupation with failure, as they made fewer statements about performance, were more highly engaged with the task, and demonstrated higher levels of emotional engagement. More importantly, the children with a learning orientation actually outperformed those with a performance orientation. Although the performance number was not statistically significant, their actual performance was about 15% higher. The researchers concluded:

> Learning goal children remained focused on strategy and maintained an even emotional keel during the hard task; they evaluated their skills positively and persisted after failure. In contrast, children with performance goals only took on challenges for which they knew they would succeed, sometimes even choosing tasks that were within reach over tasks that were easily accomplished. The researchers concluded that children with a performance orientation preferred the success task, suggesting that they were unwilling to put their professed skills to the test. This motivational pattern is potentially less adaptive than the learning goal pattern because children may forgo challenges, even some they feel able to meet.
>
> Smiley & Dweck, 1994, pp. 1739–1740

Although studies of children cannot necessarily be extrapolated to organizational contexts, these findings have been supported in research on adults as well (Seijts et al., 2004). In addition, a strong tradition of adult development (see, for example, Kegan, 1998) supports the notion that learning takes on a qualitatively different character depending on one's orientation to the problem. Adult development describes how adults transition through distinct levels of learning, in which each level requires the adult to acquire a unique set of skills, abilities, and insights. In contrast to studies that show that orientation to either learning or performance is set early in childhood, adult development and adult learning theory emphasize how orientation changes over time. Figure 3.1 illustrates the characteristics of functioning in the distinct operational orientations and operational environments.

The performance/learning orientation distinction helps to conceptualize the distinction between engaged and unengaged routine described by Cohen. When the operational context of performance/learning orientation is placed at a right angle to the routine and novelty orientation, what results is four distinct activities based on the relationship among learning, performance, and operational context. Effective navigation of the intersection between novelty

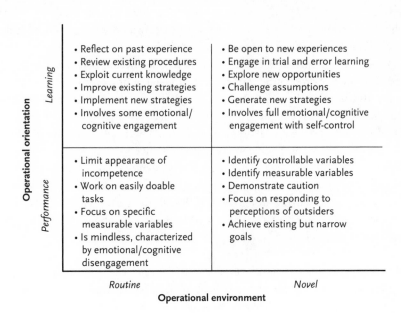

	Routine	Novel

Learning	• Reflect on past experience
	• Review existing procedures
	• Exploit current knowledge
	• Improve existing strategies
	• Implement new strategies
	• Involves some emotional/
	  cognitive engagement
		• Be open to new experiences
		• Engage in trial and error learning
		• Explore new opportunities
		• Challenge assumptions
		• Generate new strategies
		• Involves full emotional/cognitive
		  engagement with self-control

Performance	• Limit appearance of
	  incompetence
	• Work on easily doable
	  tasks
	• Focus on specific
	  measurable variables
	• Is mindless, characterized
	  by emotional/cognitive
	  disengagement
		• Identify controllable variables
		• Identify measurable variables
		• Demonstrate caution
		• Focus on responding to
		  perceptions of outsiders
		• Achieve existing but narrow
		  goals

Operational orientation (vertical axis)

Operational environment (horizontal axis)

Figure 3.1:
Performance and learning in two distinct environments.

and learning requires searching for new information, having a limited but controlled emotional engagement, and challenging assumptions. The intersection between novelty and performance requires engaged performance—identifying new variables and cause-and-effect relationships while maintaining feelings of competence and performance. The intersection between routine and performance involves performance-directed routine: emotional detachment, a focus on doable and known tasks, and improvement of existing strategies associated with task completion. The intersection between routine and learning involves learning-directed routine: exploiting current knowledge and experience, engaging in trial-and-error learning, and reflecting on current processes to create small improvements.

Figure 3.2 illustrates the shift in operational demands experienced by AF 447: As the aircraft shifted from normal law to alternate law, the crew was unprepared to deal with the challenges brought about by this shift because the shift required the team to move to a learning orientation.

The AF 447 disaster provides a window into mechanisms of learning during routine and novel situations and how learning is a distinct operational model. The crew's inability to shift from performance mode to learning mode as the aircraft shifted from normal to alternate operations led to a crucial failure in operating ability. The crisis should have been over as the team returned to routine flight after recovering from the initial stall warning brought about by the faulty pitot tube. Instead, the already anxiety-stricken Bonin continued to pull back on

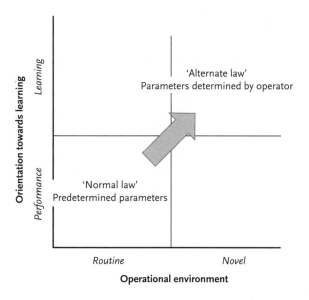

Figure 3.2:
The shift in operational demands encountered by the crew of AF 447.

the stick. The more experienced Robert, not clear in his role, failed to correctly advise the less-experienced pilot. The lack of a clear authority structure in the cockpit further contributed to an environment of uncertainty and an inability to effectively learn. The first breakdown of equipment led to the second breakdown, the breakdown of learning.

CONCLUSION

This chapter has outlined the important distinction between a learning orientation and a performance orientation and the role of these orientations in organizational breakdown. The AF 447 disaster provides an unfortunate example of the consequences that can ensue when crews fail to shift into learning mode when operational demands shift from routine to novel. The chapter suggests that learning goes beyond preparation for operations and after-action review; learning also plays a key role in operations during crisis.

SECTION II
The Breakdown of Learning

CHAPTER 4
A Review of Failure in Organizations

GROUPTHINK AND ORGANIZATIONAL FAILURE

Irving Janis (1972, 1982) remains one of the most influential scholars in the area of organizational failure. He studied the psychology of decision making and how decisions can lead to disastrous consequences. Some of the most significant threats to organizations, he noted, weren't threats that emerged from outside the organization. In other words, threats didn't emerge from factors such as disruptive technologies or changing market conditions. The most significant threats, he believed, emerged from within the organization. Janis noted that organizations often experience failure because key decision-making groups within the organization become isolated and fail to maintain critical thinking. As critical thinking erodes, groups fail to adequately consider alternatives. He called this phenomenon "groupthink" after a term devised by sociologist W. F. Whyte (1952) to describe how individuals in groups pressure each other into making decisions that reflect the dominant viewpoint of the group.

Janis later sought to apply groupthink to help government leaders improve policymaking decisions. In addition to clarifying public policy failures, Janis's theory of groupthink has been used to explain countless leadership debacles, from decision making in small groups to the largest and most complex systems. More than a theory of how the psychology of decision making can go awry, Janis's groupthink offers an explanation for why organizations often fail in their efforts to learn.

Groupthink offers an explanation for failed attempts to maintain learning, including the Bay of Pigs, the Kennedy administration's failed military takeover of Cuba by a group of Cuban exiles; the Challenger disaster, the decision to launch the space shuttle Challenger despite limited information on the risks of the launch; the Vietnam War, the use of the U.S. military to ward off the communists from South Vietnam; and more recently the lead up to and invasion of Iraq by U.S. military forces.

Imagine if this phenomenon of groupthink, in which groups limit critical thinking in order to maintain group cohesion, could explain the most significant government policy, business, and technology failures of the last three generations. Could one unified theory put to rest the vast number of conspiracy theories, partisan outcries, and overpoliticized inquiries into organizational decisions gone bad? This is the promise offered by the groupthink hypothesis.

Simply stated, the groupthink hypothesis describes how failure emerges as group members seek to stamp out critical thinking, pressure members into conforming to the dominant viewpoint within the group, and marginalize members of the group who disagree with the status quo. Cohesion is a key element of the groupthink explanation for failure. Cohesion describes how individuals seek out camaraderie in other group members. Individuals want to feel included when they enter into a group; nobody wants to be an outsider. In order to maintain group harmony and avoid being excluded from the group, individuals ally either with the dominant members or with the dominant collective position held by the group.

Janis was eager to understand the leadership dynamics that contribute to groupthink. As he studied groups making real-life decisions, he learned that groups with strong leaders tended to make poorer decisions. He noticed that groups that isolated themselves from outside opinions became unable to assess the potential downsides of a decision. The unintended consequences of a decision were often ignored. One of the reasons that groupthink has been so widely accepted is that it brings to light the psychological underpinnings of failure. Janis, as an insightful psychologist and careful researcher, identified deeply seated desires of individuals—such as the need to be part of a group, the human desire to avoid conflict, and the need for approval from superiors—as underlying causes of bad decisions.

Another reason for the popularity of groupthink is that it describes a common experience people have in groups. Individuals have an inherent psychological need to feel a sense of belonging. Individual identity emerges from group membership (see Turner & Pratkanis, 1999a,b). When working in a group, people often feel pressure to conform, develop anxieties about their participation, and become uncomfortable for fear of being excluded. This means that challenging the viewpoints held by key members of a group or organization can be risky. No person wants to be seen as a troublemaker or be accused of not being a team player. Even more alarming, people may feel that leaders rely on the groupthink effect as a subtle form of control.

THE LIMITS OF GROUPTHINK

Groupthink also addresses how people learn, although the link between groupthink and learning is not always obvious. Groupthink reminds us that learning is not always about rational thinking; rather, learning in organizations can be confounded by the psychology of politics and power (Vince, 1998). Janis's group-think reminds us that, at the core, learning may be grounded in human desire, frailty, and irrational belief.

Many organizations take steps to counter groupthink only to find that they have the opposite effect. One way organizations seek to counteract groupthink is by appointing someone to play devil's advocate. The notion that someone should play the role of devil's advocate, a person to take an opposing position to the dominant viewpoint, originated with the Catholic Church. The devil's advocate, or *advocatus diaboli* in Latin, was charged with taking the opposing or dissenting view in the canonization process of determining sainthood.

One organization often criticized for its groupthink-like mentality took steps to counteract the groupthink effect. It put to task one of Janis's recommenda-tions and established a devil's advocate role within the organization. It appointed an individual to take an opposing stance to the dominant viewpoint. The dev-il's advocate had its intended effect and critical thinking was increased, but the implementation of a devil's advocate had an unintended effect. The arguing and confrontation brought about by the devil's advocate role only enhanced the dominant position. The group's conviction became stronger, and they held even tighter to their existing beliefs. Group leaders adapted their message to counter the criticisms of the devil's advocate. Cohesion increased and the organization continued along the same path, despite the open and institutionalized dissent. The end effect turned out to be the opposite of what the organization had sought.

When attempts like this, designed to limit groupthink, only serve to delay the onset of groupthink, we can see the power of peer pressure in groups. The failure to counter groupthink in this organization also exposes a limitation with many of the other approaches to explain organizational failure. Janis's concept of groupthink grounds organizational failure in the basic human psychologi-cal need for acceptance and esprit-de-corps. Janis's work is grounded in the assumption that individuals working in groups resolve anxiety by conforming to group pressure. Thus, as t'Hart, Stern, and Sundelious (1997) have argued, groupthink emphasizes a somewhat limited aspect of group decision making.

Too many explanations of why organizations fail, fail the usefulness test because they address only limited aspects of failure. Single-dimensional expla-nations tempt leaders and other problem solvers to rely on overly simplified solu-tions. Systematic research on groupthink (see Tetlock, McGuire, Peterson, Feld, & Chang, 1992), for example, reveals a problem with applying the groupthink hypothesis in practice. Recall that an important element of groupthink is group cohesion; cohesive groups are thought to make bad decisions. However, system-atic research shows that group cohesion can result in both good and bad deci-sions. It turns out that groupthink, or at least the presence of its core ingredient, cohesion, doesn't distinguish between good and bad decisions.

Groupthink, in many ways, is the standard by which all considerations of organizational failure should be measured. The theory is based on underlying assumptions of human behavior that have stood the test of time: peer pressure and its impact on actions of group members. Further, that groups often exert dysfunctional pressure on group members to perform offers a practical guide to help leaders, managers, and groups themselves make better decisions and improve performance. Like every theory in the study of organizations, the groupthink explanation of organizational failure also has limitations. Groups that display characteristics of groupthink do not always come to dysfunctional decisions as the theory suggests. Further, the concept of groupthink provides a limited lens through which to view organizational failure. Like other theories of failure I explore in this chapter, the underlying assumptions of groupthink both (1) support the theory's underlying explanatory power, and (2) reveal the limits of the theory. By reviewing both the strengths and weaknesses of various theories, we can develop a better understanding of both the value of existing approaches to failure and their limitations. Next, I turn to the foundational concept of organizational intelligence, which has the distinction of being, perhaps, the first systematic explanation for the breakdown of learning in organizations. A summary of explanations for organizational failure can be found in Table 4.1.

Table 4.1. DESCRIPTIONS, DEFINITIONS, AND MECHANISMS FOR FAILURE IN ORGANIZATIONS

Primary mechanism of failure	Representative theory or description	Definition of failure
Group process	Groupthink	Group norms of cohesiveness increase conformity and limit critical thinking
Information handling	Organizational intelligence	Organizations are unable to properly interpret and handle information
Culture	Stages of failure	Certain cultural norms no longer prove adequate and require readjustment
Organizational complexity	Normal accident theory	The more complex and more highly coupled a task, the more likely a small deviation from normal operations can lead to a failure
System coordination	High-reliability organizations	Individuals can no longer make collective cognitive sense of interactions or the context in which they take place
Improper goals or means	Human error	Planned actions fail to achieve their desired goals, or there are "unsuccessful experiments in an unfriendly environment"
Expertise	Integrative-cognitive complexity	Members of the organization fail to understand the complexity of a situation with enough detail to discern the true underlying problems
Adaptation	Behavioral organization decision making	There is inadequate exploitation of existing knowledge or exploration of new knowledge opportunities

ORGANIZATIONAL INTELLIGENCE

Harold Wilensky (1967) presented learning in organizations as a somewhat systematic process. He focused on the nature of information, what he referred to as "organizational intelligence." In contrast to Janis's psychological-social approach, Wilensky believed that organizational failure arises from the inability of organizations to properly gather, process, interpret, and communicate information. Failure occurs because organizations have ineffective policies and procedures for how they handle, route, and interpret information. Systematic failure, therefore, is likely the result of poorly designed and executed policies and procedures. He believed that with proper organizational intelligence, organizations can avoid, forestall, or more adequately respond to failure. Proper organizational intelligence should be "clear, timely, reliable, valid, adequate and wide ranging" (Wilensky, 1967, p. 121).

Several specific problems arise in interpreting and handling information. An information clarity problem arises when information cannot be understood in a way that informs proper action. Reliability failure emerges when there is a lack of consensus on how to interpret information; in other words, information could be seen in different ways by different observers. An information failure due to problems with validity emerges from the failure of information to appropriately capture reality, as when it captures only part, but not the whole story. Failures of scope result from inadequate interpretation, in which analysts fail to view alternatives and misread information.

Wilensky's typology provided some of the first insights into how vulnerability arises due to lack of intelligence. With the increasing reliance on knowledge as the basis for organizational success, the notion of an intelligence failure becomes relevant to all organizations. Wilensky believed that intelligence failures were more the norm than the exception. The complex, dynamic, and human nature of organizations makes them vulnerable to intelligence failures. He argued that "intelligence failures are rooted in structural problems that cannot be fully solved; they express universal dilemmas of organizational life that can, however, be resolved in various ways at varying costs" (1967, p. 42).

Like the groupthink hypothesis, the intelligence approach provides a starting point to further understand failure in organizations more broadly. Wilensky contributed a working typology for organizational vulnerability. First, vulnerability emerges from a failure in goal setting, which results from a crisis in purpose, mission, or direction. Second, vulnerability of controls emerges due to failure in securing compliance with rules, as with lapses in policies and in compliance. Similar lapses in control could occur due to leadership, authority, coordination, incentives, information, or group dynamics. A third form of vulnerability arises due to innovation, brought about by a failure to adapt to changing circumstances. The fourth vulnerability arises due to poorly handled or unavailable information. Information vulnerability threatens organizations most of all, but the threat of information often goes unrecognized, so Wilensky focused much of his attention on problems of information (p. viii).

Despite its influence, Wilensky's approach also remains incomplete because the hypothesis falls short in several important areas. For example, Wilensky failed to consider that interpretations of knowledge are always shaped by power, and which interpretation is considered correct will always be due, in some part or large part, to those who control the interpretation (Clegg et al., 2006). Similarly, intelligence can seldom be viewed as objective. Rather, in order to understand intelligence, organizations need to understand how cultural and political forces shape interpretations. What is considered a correct interpretation of information will always emerge from an individual's point of view (Nonaka, 1994).

More contemporary analysis of organizational intelligence failure comes from SK Group Consulting (Probst & Raisch, 2005). They analyzed 100 of the top business crises between 2000 and 2005 and identified two primary reasons for organizational failure. One reason was the burnout syndrome. The burnout syndrome occurs because organizations pursue too much of what is normally considered a good thing: too much growth, too much change, too much success, and even too much positive leadership! The problem is that each of these seemingly positive aspects of organizational culture can lead to burnout. In the study, burnout arose from internal factors such as competition for resources, mistrust, an overly positive vision, the prior success of the company, actions taken by leaders, or organizational growth fueled by unsustainable factors such as taking on too much debt. The other reason for failure was what the researchers termed "premature aging." This meant that the organizations were not engaging in enough success factors. The companies seemed content with stagnating growth, were tentative about change, were content with weak organizational leadership, and lacked a culture geared toward success.

ORGANIZATIONAL CULTURE

Turner (1976) criticized Wilensky's approach on practical grounds. He argued that the idealized or normative view of intelligence offered by Wilensky provided little guidance for those working with real-world problems. Turner instead turned to the concept of culture to define failure as a situation in which certain cultural norms no longer prove adequate and require readjustment. He outlined six distinct stages (p. 381) to a crisis based on cultural norms, and I add a seventh.

- Stage 1 is described as normal operating procedures. In this phase, cultural norms and routine ways of doing business are functional and able to prevent failure. These norms provide a foundation for coordination of organizational goals and may even foster success. Looking at policies, procedures, espoused values, and artifacts can identify norms.

- Stage 2 is the incubation period. During the incubation phase, a series of events occurs in which the norms do not function as they had in the past. The dysfunctional aspects of the norms begin to emerge but go largely unnoticed by leadership. The incubation period is crucial because the norms are commingled with existing routines and the rigidity of the routines makes the norms difficult to change; strong norms make it difficult to accept information that contradicts their effectiveness.
- Stage 3 is the stage of precipitating events. During this phase, the first events of the failure begin to surface and, if attended to by organizational leaders, the events can lead to the challenge of norms or development of new norms. Organizations are particularly vulnerable because during this stage, members are likely to spot problems with current practices, but often withdraw from changing them because they find other explanations for why things are not going well.
- Stage 4 involves the onset of failure, in which the "immediate consequences of the collapse of cultural precautions become apparent" (p. 381).
- Stage 5 is the rescue and salvage stage. This stage requires an immediate response that is designed to do one of three things: contain the failure, limit its impact, or begin its recovery.
- Stage 6 involves cultural adjustment. Many organizations never reach this stage. This requires a re-evaluation and shift in cultural norms. New models of how the organization works (or fails) emerge, and new norms are developed and infused in the culture throughout the organization. In this phase, the organization begins to redefine the nature of the problem and take precautions to avoid future failures.
- Stage 7 involves industrywide assessment and adjustment. In this stage, lessons learned are disseminated across an industry, and industrywide norms associated with the prevention of future failure are established (see, for example, Ameli & Kayes, 2011).

Turner concluded that culture can lead to failure in several ways. Failure occurs because assumptions about the nature of how things work are incorrect, which in turn results in a failure to correctly assess a situation. Another reason failure emerges is the inability to handle and interpret information. Because most organizational goals are ill structured, there are multiple possible paths to achieve these goals. Further, failure can result from not following rules, by systematically ignoring safety violations or other regulations or rules that stabilize a system. Most importantly, failure can result from an emergent anxiety or fear over potential outcomes. In observing disasters, Turner noticed that many organizational failures could be attributed to a kind of willful ignorance, in which organizational leaders failed to act in early phases of a failure. Ignoring the early warning signs was justified by (a) treating the warning signs as ambiguous and therefore not actionable, (b) giving specific and important warning signs low priority, or (c) completely ignoring the sign due to psychological disposition.

NORMAL ACCIDENT THEORY

Normal accident theory (NAT) takes a sociological approach to understanding organizational failure. The NAT perspective is most closely associated with Charles Perrow (1999), who described how the interaction between complexity and task coupling can lead to small deviations in normal operating procedure. The complexity of a task is a function of its number of elements and the dynamic nature of those elements. The more dimensions to the task, the more likely something can go wrong. Coupling is a function of how closely one task is related to another task. In a closely coupled system, a deviation in one small task can quickly spread to another part of the organization. In a loosely coupled system, the parts are less interconnected; deviations in one aspect of a task do not quickly affect another part of the organization.

Organizational failure is linked to coupling and complexity. The more complex and more highly coupled a task, the more likely a small deviation from normal operations can lead to a larger system failure. Under this thinking, a small deviation from routine operation, even a deviation that would be expected under normal conditions, can quickly escalate into unanticipated events. Technology is the core ingredient of failure according to the NAT approach. In a complex system, even a simple event, such as the weather pattern, can escalate out of control because one event is closely linked (or coupled) to other events. Complex systems are quite vulnerable, even during normal operating procedures. Failures are not simply rare events; they are certain to happen. The link between NAT and learning is that organizational learning processes may help individuals recognize these small deviations and take prompt action before they grow into a full-scale organizational failure. Further, if learning does break down, then those within the organization need to respond to the crisis once it has erupted. The NAT perspective insists that no matter how much learning goes on within an organization, the organization remains at constant risk of breakdown and crisis because breakdowns are a normal function of operating in a complex, dynamic, and high-risk environment.

Normal accident theory provides a powerful model. It is helpful to think of organizations as complex and it is also theoretically interesting; however, complexity is difficult to grasp experientially. Like other approaches discussed, NAT is abstract, leaving both researchers and practitioners wanting to find answers on how to respond to or address failure in practice.

The research on high-reliability organizations (HROs) directly addresses the role of experience and more actively indicates how to address failures—before they grow out of control. Although groupthink relies on assumptions about human psychology and NAT rests on sociological assumptions, HRO is based on assumptions about interpersonal interaction. The HRO approach in organizational studies is most closely linked with Karl Weick (1993, 1995; Weick, Sutcliffe, & Obstfeld, 1999) and Karlene Roberts (Weick & Roberts, 1993) and their essays on how individuals within organizations make sense of particular situations. They describe how organizations piece together "sense" by coordinating interpretations of the environment. These interpretations emerge through interactions. Failure emerges when individuals can no longer make collective cognitive sense of these interactions or the context in which they take place. Organizational failure emerges when sensemaking deteriorates in the face of increasingly senseless situations.

High-reliability organizations ward off breakdown by building five values into daily practice: (1) sensitivity to operations, (2) commitment to resilience, (3) deference to experience, (4) reluctance to simplify, and (5) preoccupation with failure. This first value is sensitivity to operations. This includes an understanding and focus on "what if" scenarios; a focus on concrete experience; an orientation toward operations rather than adherence to abstract principles; and careful attention to detail. Commitment to resilience involves the ability to respond to localized errors before they turn into large systematic problems. Deference to experience requires relying on those who work directly with technology and other experts who can provide insight from a variety of different perspectives. Those involved in HROs also show a reluctance to simplify by continuing to develop new and complex scenarios and models of how things work. Finally, HROs hold a preoccupation with failure in that they focus almost obsessive attention on collecting, reporting, and analyzing problems and errors.

La Porte's (1988) description of the U.S. air traffic control system describes how HROs work:

> An air traffic [sub]system is largely a mental rather than a physical construct. It has no visible, concrete supporting connectors. The system must be "seen in the head," a mental construct recognized by thousands of people [controllers, pilots, facilities managers] in order for "it" to be operative. (p. 223)

The HRO perspective moves us closer to understanding the role that direct experience plays in failure because it reveals that learning is a process of interpretation, not a process based on probability, as Karl Weick (1993, 1995) has so eloquently explained. However, the HRO approach continues to be skeptical about the role of experience and learning in building HROs (see, for example, Vogus, Sutcliffe, & Weick, 2010, p. 68). Although the HRO approach and a learning approach share concerns about cognitive processes and interpretations (e.g., Daft & Weick, 1984), the HRO approach draws on a different set of assumptions about the nature of learning because it says little about the specific emotions or experiences that emerge during a situation. In summary, research on HRO that occurs within the study of organizations emphasizes the cognitive aspects of intrateam and interteam coordination rather than direct experience.

HUMAN ERROR

The human error approach to failure focuses on error, which is a deviation from expectation. The human error approach, also called the human factors approach, offers a goal-based formula in which failure emerges because things have not gone as planned. Most notable is the work of James Reason. He viewed failure in terms of human errors that emerge when planned actions fail to achieve their desired goals (1990, pp. 5–8). Things can go wrong either because the plan was wrong or because something went wrong during the execution of the plan. The human error approach makes an important distinction between error and violation. An error is not intentional, but rather is related to a mistake; something simply did not go as planned. On the other hand, a violation involves a social context, and the act goes against a prescribed rule. Rasmussen (1982) provided another dimension to failure that considers both internal psychological factors as well as factors within the environment. He described failures as "unsuccessful experiments in an unfriendly environment" (Isaac et al., 2002, p. 37).

Taken together, Rasmussen and Reason offer a three-dimensional model of organizational failure based on any or all of the dimensions of skills, rules, and knowledge. Skill-based failure arises from the lack of skill in performing a task. A skill-based failure is usually tacit, in that the individuals do not have a grasp on the failure they experience. A rule-based failure emerges when the wrong rule is applied during the course of operation. This type of failure is often procedural in the sense that the operator applies a known rule but applies it wrong, or fails to apply the correct rule. Thus, a rule-based failure is usually more explicit, more observable. Finally, a knowledge-based mistake emerges due to a failure to understand a situation—either because the operator fails to adequately understand the situation or because there is not a clear understanding of how to proceed. This type of failure often occurs when prior knowledge of a situation is limited. In some cases, a knowledge-based failure can emerge because the operator does not have the knowledge, but in many cases the knowledge domain itself is incomplete and an adequate understanding of a system has not yet been developed.

The study of errors provides a systems-based approach to failure, but its value in understanding organizational failure is complicated by a few additional considerations. The first complication is often referred to as the "sharp edge of the knife" problem. In the case of many organizational failures, it is easier to find an explanation for a failure closer to the crisis or deviation itself. This is a problem because in the case of most failures, latent factors are also involved. Latent factors are underlying factors such as organizational culture that cannot be directly attributed to specific acts, but can lay dormant for years. Most failures involve both latent and active factors. The human error approach offers important contributions to how we understand failure in organizations, but the perspective is also limited by its mechanistic view.

ORGANIZATIONAL ADAPTATION

James March (1991) identified two important processes for learning that are relevant for understanding organizational failure: exploration and exploitation. March's approach to organizational learning is based largely on an organizational learning model associated with environmental adaptation. Organizations learn through exploration when they seek out new forms of knowledge, opportunities, and innovations. A second way that organizations learn is through exploitation. Exploitation occurs when organizations rely on existing resources and knowledge to develop new opportunities. Exploration and exploitation are two basic functions that are essential for the survival of any organization. March's dimensions of exploration and exploitation provide the foundation for understanding the basic processes of learning in organizations. Under this definition, organizational failure emerges due to the inability to exploit existing opportunities or to explore new opportunities for knowledge. Despite the influence of the exploitation and exploration model, its origins fail to or in some cases outright reject the role of experience (March, 2011), in turn, relying on abstract notions that miss significant elements of the learning equation.

COGNITIVE COMPLEXITY AND EXPERTISE

Phillip Tetlock's (1994) model of integrative complexity, like the HRO approach, also focuses on cognitive aspects of organizational failure. Integrative complexity, as a form of cognitive complexity, involves the ability to process large amounts of information and to assess that information from various perspectives. Cognitive complexity describes a series of progressive steps in which each new step is marked by an improved ability to process information in a more complex and, therefore, more complete way. As individuals climb to increasingly higher levels of cognitive complexity, they improve their ability to manage multiple goals or respond to a diverse set of stakeholders. In contemporary organizations, in which information processing and complex knowledge are a requirement for success, improved cognitive complexity can improve an organization's ability to perform. From the perspective of cognitive complexity, organizational failures emerge because the members of the organization fail to understand the complexity of a situation with enough detail to discern the true underlying problems. Decision makers fail to understand their own assumptions and the conditions under which their decision making holds (Tetlock & Mellers, 2011).

Cognitive complexity involves developing two cognitive-based abilities, differentiation and integration. Differentiation involves finding differences between two ideas, whereas integration involves finding similarities between two seemingly different ideas. A person who improves in cognitive complexity improves the ability to differentiate and integrate ideas. These two abilities exist on seven distinct levels. At the highest level of cognitive complexity, the individual is no longer bound by existing rules but recognizes the limitations of current thinking, understands more macro and micro factors that impact events, and considers multiple factors when assessing a situation. At the highest level of cognitive complexity, the individual holds an overarching view of how things work and is able to express that perspective with great detail. He or she takes a global view, taking into account multiple perspectives, even if these are later rejected based on reasoned thinking. Importantly, at the highest level of cognitive thinking, the individual recognizes trade-offs and unintended consequences of events.

Tetlock's approach to cognitive complexity has been applied to leaders and their decision making, including former U.S. Presidents Bill Clinton, Jimmy Carter, and George W. Bush (Conway, Suedfeld, & Tetlock, 2000) and Winston Churchill (Tetlock & Tyler, 1996). The model of cognitive complexity has also been used to describe decision making in the Supreme Court, in policy decisions, and in business.

Despite the advantages of an approach to organizational failure based on critical thinking, such as the model offered by Tetlock, cognitive approaches like the integrative complexity model present problems when applied to organizational contexts. They often discount the emotional aspects of decision making in favor of cognitive aspects. In contrast, experience-based models emphasize cognition, action, and emotion. Experience-based learning is also different from expert learning because expert learning is always domain specific. Experts excel at specific domains such as chess, music, or writing. Experience-based learning may also be domain specific, but the domains are more broadly defined in terms of problem structure, knowledge structure, and routine. Expert learning is associated with well-structured problems, whereas experience-based learning requires action in both routine situations and in situations that are nonroutine. When faced with a learning situation that involves multiple information processing capacities, multiple learning approaches are needed.

CONCLUSION

This chapter has reviewed perspectives on failure in organizations. Explanations for failure in organizations have been offered at the individual, group, organizational, and sociological levels. There are a broad range of assumptions about the nature of failure, including an emphasis on cognition, task and system complexity, and deviation from expected or desired goals. Although not a comprehensive review of the understanding of failure, this chapter has provided an introduction to the diversity of explanations directed at how failure arises in organizations.

This chapter has discussed several considerations for why organizations fail, which, taken together, offer a better understanding of the causes and consequences of failure. Although existing perspectives offer deep insights into the nature of failure in organizations, at times the variety of perspectives can appear confusing, even contradictory, and can quickly overwhelm those looking to forestall, respond, and recover from failure. The multitude of different assumptions underlying theses perspectives only contribute to the confusion. For example, although the HRO perspective focuses on interactions between individual actors and rests primarily on assumptions of social psychology, the NAT framework places the cause of failure at a systems level and rests on sociological assumptions. In another set of seeming contradictions, the human error approach assumes that, on some level, all organizations function in a rational way, whereas the culture approach assumes the opposite: that organizations are embedded in consistent but often irrational beliefs and routines. Although an extensive amount of research contributes to a better understanding of failure, a more complete understanding of failure requires consideration of learning in organizations, which is the subject of the next chapter.

CHAPTER 5

From Failure to the Breakdown of Learning

WHAT LEARNING THEORY CAN TEACH US ABOUT ORGANIZATIONAL RESILIENCE

When an organization takes seriously the role of learning from prior breakdowns and builds learning into its everyday routines, organizations become more resilient. How individuals in organizations learn, and what happens when they stop learning, is key to understanding resilience. This chapter further explores how learning plays a key role in day-to-day operations of organizations. Learning impacts operations across different levels of the organization, and learning offers insights into unexplored aspects of failure such as identity, anxiety, and shifting routines.

The likelihood that an organization learns is enhanced when it engages in some of the following processes:

- Collecting and retaining information on experiences, near misses, and counterfactual experiences that have occurred within the organization, among competitors, and within the organization's industry
- Identifying and addressing the blind spots and assumptions that emerge from past successes and failure
- Monitoring compensation-based incentives, vision and goals, and human capital practices
- Recognizing and preparing for second-order or unintended consequences of decisions
- Attending to systems that overtax resources, create unnecessary stress, and generate unmanageable risks

The last chapter reviewed frameworks for understanding failure in organizations. This chapter provides an alternative conceptualization of failure: Much of what constitutes failure in organizations can be understood as a breakdown in learning. The word "breakdown" implies a double meaning. The first meaning denotes the inability to maintain functional or working order. It implies a quick or sudden loss in ability. In the Air France Flight 447 breakdown, the crew lost its ability to function and respond to events in a timely manner such that by the time it recovered and began learning, the team was unable to recover. The second meaning of breakdown denotes a process of analyzing or classifying distinct parts of a process. Decomposing or dissecting the events facilitate a better understanding of what occurred. In both meanings, the process of breakdown is itself a source of learning. It is through breakdown—breaking the experiences into their constituent parts, analyzing and reflecting upon them—that we can begin to learn from them. Breakdown, then, is itself another step toward learning: Learning doesn't begin or end with the events; learning begins well before the events, may continue during the events, and is the key source of resilience in the aftermath of events.

With the two aspects of breakdown in mind, breakdown, better than other terms, connotes a sense of something working well that changes course or direction. The implication is that under most conditions, learning is a default position in that it is a natural part of organizational functioning. What must be studied, then, is not the process of failure, but how learning moves from a naturally occurring process to one that no longer seems to occur.

The term does carry a mechanical overtone, in the sense that "breakdown" is often used to describe mechanical processes such as a car breakdown, a machinery breakdown, or even a communication breakdown. In a behavioral context, as opposed to a mechanical context, breakdown has its origins in psychology as it describes how a normally functioning person stops functioning in a normal way. In this context, the term is used generally rather than referencing to a particular mental disorder or medical situation. Breakdown is a useful term because experts and nonexperts can rely on it to communicate individual experience and thus begin to address, in practical ways, situations they encounter. The nonexpert use of the term may imply that something is going on that deserves greater attention, without knowledge of the specific problem or the ability to isolate a specific cause or event. Thus, the term "breakdown" promises to be quite useful to a range of people, both experts and nonexperts, with a variety of experiences and in a variety of positions throughout the organization because it is a nontechnical term invoked to signal a shift from normal to subnormal processes (Rapport, Todd, Lumley, & Fisicaro, 1998). To refer to a breakdown in learning is to refer to either technical or nontechnical circumstances, useful to a variety of people working in organizations (World Encyclopedia, 2012).

A breakdown in learning implies three aspects of the experience that are both time-bound and specific. The result is an uneasiness or anxiety founded upon one or more experiences of the following three scenarios. In one scenario, the individual finds himself stuck, which may result from the inability to resolve a learning dilemma (say, for example, the inability to decide between using reflective observation or active experimentation). In a second scenario, an individual finds herself experiencing a situation in which learning demands exceed her learning capacity, perhaps due to the novel nature of the experience or the developmental nature of the experience. In a third scenario, the individual finds herself unable to process information. The knowledge gathering and processing mechanisms of learning become stifled, perhaps due to situational circumstances, lack of prior experience, or an inability to move from routine to novelty.

Experiential learning serves as the basis for this conceptualization. Kolb (1984) described the transformative aspects of learning. Learning is a natural process of gathering and processing knowledge. In developing this description of learning, Kolb emphasized that learning is a continual process, and under the best conditions, learning results in transformation of knowledge. Later theoretical contributions revealed some of the factors that might block learning. For example, Vince (1998) and Vince and Reynolds (2004), writing from a psychodynamics perspective, described how the failure to resolve learning dilemmas can result in the build up of anxiety, which further stifles learning. Hunt (1987) approached the breakdown of learning from a counseling and psychotherapy perspective and described how the failure to resolve learning dilemmas results in stifled progress in human development.

LEARNING: BEFORE, DURING, AND AFTER BREAKDOWN

One reason that breakdown, rather than failure, provides a more useful framework is because learning enters the equation well before any breakdown actually begins. Learning processes help navigate breakdown across multiple stages—before, during, and after breakdown. Smith and Elliott (2007) described the importance of learning across these three different stages of crisis. In the first stage, the learner copes with the potential demands of breakdown through training and development efforts designed to address breakdown. In this stage, the teams develop a better understanding of the learning process. One example of how learning can prepare teams for breakdowns can be found in Wilson, Burke, Priest, and Salas (2005; see also Burke et al., 2011). Noting that organizational success is built on a foundation of highly trained teams, they outlined specific training interventions that can be used to develop such teams to improve response to problems and failures. These interventions include cross-training across different functions, perceptual contrast training, coordination training similar to that received by airline pilots, self-correction training in which teams are taught to analyze the effectiveness and effects of their own behaviors, scenario-based training in which teams learn from a diverse set of cases, and guided error training in which teams learn how to self-correct small errors based on feedback from experts.

In the second stage, the learner continues to learn during normal operating procedures. Learning isn't simply present when individuals prepare to deal with breakdown; learning plays a central role in organizational operations as well. Learning improves the effectiveness of the response to different aspects of failure because it helps uncover how individuals within organizations deal with increasing complexity and novelty while simultaneously dealing with decreased predictability. Learning also plays an important role in the third stage of breakdown, as the learner seeks to identify lessons learned in the aftermath of the breakdown. Learning helps individuals understand the breakdown and how to develop an effective response in the future.

Figure 5.1 illustrates a four stage model of learning breakdown that builds on Turner's (1976) model of organizational and interorganizational disaster. The model is based on Kayes, Allen, and Self's (2013) integration of management learning with organizational disaster research and suggested that organizational resilience is a function of an organization's abilities to manage shifts in learning across four stages of breakdown. The first stage is incubation and tracks closely, Turner's stage of cultural incubation of a disaster. The second stage involved precursor events, also similar to Turner. The third stage differs from Turners in that learning itself breaks down so that the organization can no longer maintain its natural stage of learning. Only after the organization shifts to the fourth stage of rebuilding does learning become restored. Learning, better than other constructs, also provides insight into breakdown at different levels of the organization

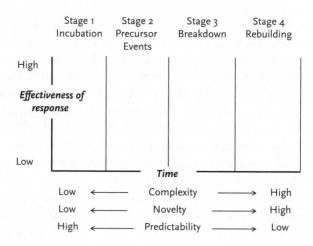

Figure 5.1:
Stages of learning breakdown.

Table 5.1. REPRESENTATIVE LEARNING ACTIVITIES ASSOCIATED
WITH DIFFERENT LEVELS AND STAGES OF CRISIS

	Incubation	Precursor events	Breakdown	Rebuilding
Organization/ industry	Strategic scenario planning, continuity planning, situational awareness	Error detection, gathering, publication	Building a safety culture at the system level, knowledge sharing	Lessons learned databases
Group	Simulations	Psychological safety	Team coordination training, team learning	After-action review
Individual	Knowledge, skills, and abilities training	Building learning orientation	Crisis response training, cognitive readiness training	Debriefs, lessons learned interviews

(Crossan, Mauer, & White, 2011). Table 5.1 identifies representative learning processes associated with different levels and stages of the crisis cycle.

IDENTITY AND LEARNING

In addition to its role at various stages and levels of organizational functioning and breakdown, learning opens up analysis of breakdown to a broader range of factors than have previously been considered under previous conceptualizations of organizational failure. Fraher (2004), for example, has made inroads in applying concepts of identity and the related cognitive, social, emotional, and economic demands placed on commercial airline pilots in the post 9/11 airline industry and how these factors threatened airline safety. She argued that our understanding of the potential for failure requires a broader understanding of human interaction. Researchers must stretch beyond task-related factors such as the technical aspects involved in flying a plane and grasp underlying issues associated with how individuals learn, the identities that shape individual thinking, and the emotions involved in responding to dramatic task and social demands. A more complete understanding of how a crew of pilots operates requires consideration of how pilots construct their identity, deal with anxiety, and relate to others both in and out of the cockpit.

Much of the research on identity has the flavor of learning, but terminology from the fields of learning is seldom invoked. For example, Ibarra's (1999) study of identity formation in young professionals recognized the power of learning from experience without mentioning it explicitly. In fact, the words "experience" and "learning" never appeared in her study, despite the fact that she attributed socialization in young professionals to processes associated with observing, experimenting, and evaluating. Perhaps the oversight of learning occurs in research like this because the study is embedded in the context of culture, socialization, and work transition rather than learning, and thus focuses on the external factors that influence behaviors rather than the emotional, cognitive, and habitual factors that allow individuals to manage the experiences associated with strong socialization pressures. What Ibarra's work represents is that those interested in understanding learning may have something to gain from studies of identity once that research is embedded in conceptualizations of identity consistent with learning and human development (e.g., Erikson, 1956).

CONCLUSION

The chapter has emphasized the importance of experience and the ability to learn from experience as a key factor in organizational resilience. Drawing on prior research on experiential learning, the breakdown of learning in organizations is offered as an additional consideration for why organizations fail because it better captures the experience of what occurs in organizations during failure. When individuals within a system learn to prepare, respond, and recovery from breakdown systematic resilience begins. The next two chapters explore two unlikely factors that facilitate the breakdown of learning.

CHAPTER 6

How Optimism and Positive Thinking Can Limit Learning

LEARNING FROM THE COLLAPSE OF ENRON

Until the breakdown of Lehman Brothers in 2008, the single largest bankruptcy in history lay at the hands of a few overly optimistic executives at a company called Enron. Enron represents one of the worst-case scenarios associated with the breakdown of learning in organizations. As others who have studied the events have already noted, deception, arrogance, greed, and even fraud led to the collapse, but another set of factors was lurking alongside these psychological processes: an unbridled optimism that threatened learning.

Enron was a pioneer in the natural gas industry. Many companies and analysts admired the firm's management team for turning the rather stodgy and predictable business of natural gas production, storage, and transfer into a fast trading, highly profitable business. Through years of diligent work, Enron had built a substantial network of natural gas pipelines across the United States. Later it moved into trading electric utilities and other commodities in addition to natural gas. For two of the top leaders at Enron, Ken Lay and Jeff Skilling, the day-to-day business of natural gas became too predictable. They believed that government regulation stifled profits and growth and that they had identified a better way to do business.

Few knew more about the natural gas industry and few believed in its potential more than Ken Lay. Ken Lay, Enron's president and an economist by training, spent most of his professional career fighting to create a market-driven natural gas market. Skilling, on the other hand, had no real interest in the industry itself. He was focused almost exclusively on profits. In his life before Enron, Skilling was a high-profile consultant and had helped several companies realize their full potential by adopting the latest management practices. Lay hired Skilling to do the same at Enron.

Despite their differences, Lay and Skilling did share something in common. They shared optimism. They believed that if a positive future could be imagined, that positive future could be achieved. Both executives wanted Enron to become the biggest energy company in the United States. They hoped Enron would become the largest and most profitable utility in the world. At one point, their hopes became reality. In the 1990s, natural gas prices became deregulated and Enron served as the central trading hub for the entire natural gas industry. Because Enron's management realized, sooner than others, that natural gas prices could be traded like other commodities, they built an extensive trading infrastructure. Enron soon became the natural gas broker to the world. Nearly any company wanting to do business in natural gas in the United States had to go through Enron.

Following deregulation, optimism was high as natural gas prices continued to rise. Enron profited. The company's early success earned Lay, Skilling, and other executives in the company large bonuses and recognition from their peers. Other firms began to admire Enron, not only because of its profits, but because of its progressive management practices. A *Fortune* magazine poll ranked Enron as the most admired company in the United States for six years in a row. Lay and Skilling's optimism appeared to be paying off in reputation capital as well as financial capital.

Enron profited handsomely from the newly regulated natural gas market. As the two key players guiding Enron's success, Lay and Skilling seemed so confident in their own management skill and remained so optimistic about the future prospects of the company that they primed investors to continue to expect strong returns. Skilling knew, of course, that when investors expected returns and these expectations weren't met, the unmet expectations could result in falling stock prices. Despite the problem of setting expectations too high, the Enron team expressed only optimism for Enron's future.

MANAGEMENT PRACTICES THAT LIMIT LEARNING: OPTIMISM AND SHORT-TERM GOALS

The optimism shared by the executive team at Enron resulted from an underlying sense of confidence about themselves as managers. The executives at Enron believed in their own management wizardry. The Enron team could have carefully considered their early successes and marked these successes to the unique market conditions that arose from deregulation—Enron was the first to capture the newly deregulated natural gas market. Instead, the leaders at Enron attributed their early successes to their own cleverness and management acumen. In some ways, Lay and Skilling were right. Their ability to anticipate and profit from deregulation proved to be a highly profitable business strategy.

Unfortunately, many of their management practices achieved only short-term results. They still lacked an effective long-term management strategy. At Enron, there were significant incentives for signing new deals, but there were few incentives for actually implementing the projects. Enron's biggest contracts never earned the company a penny of revenue because Enron was not able to deliver on big projects. Enron traded on its reputation as an innovator and a company with progressive management practices. Despite its reputation, Enron's management simply never developed or cultivated the expertise to build large electricity-generating plants, even though it was able to sell multibillion-dollar contracts that promised just such an outcome. In the end, Enron sacrificed its long-term viability as a company for short-term gains.

Enron's original profits might be attributed to no more than a good gamble. As the old saying goes, nothing is worse than a gambler who wins. Enron executives fell prey to a common psychological problem, attributing success to skill rather than luck. The successful gamble led to a more pressing problem. Underlying these management practices was an optimism that seemed detached from the reality of the business environment. Enron's early successes created an expectation that the success should continue. The realities of business dictate that few companies can sustain these large profits for long. Lay and Skilling's unbridled optimism and lack of self awareness would claim many victims.

THE PROBLEM OF PATHOLOGICAL OPTIMISM IN MANAGEMENT

The most significant victim was the organization's culture. Built on values like excessive risk taking and weak oversight and compliance, Enron's culture became unproductive The company's optimism didn't help the company make better decisions. The culture of optimism actually put the company at risk, a risk that ultimately led to the company's bankruptcy.

Few managers, in general, will look at optimism as a problem. After all, optimism leads to success according to many management and leadership experts. This sense of optimism, however, can threaten learning because optimism tends to stifle serious self-reflection. In the case of Enron, confidence and optimism in its own future set the stage for the company's senior officials to justify deceptive accounting practices and led to manage earnings to a predefined target.

Enron's executives may have displayed what psychologists call pathological optimism. Pathological optimism occurs when an individual holds such a strong sense of optimism about the future that it prevents him or her from recognizing current problems. Ultimately, the individual forgoes dealing with current problems by maintaining his or her optimism—thus, the pathological aspect of the optimism (Akhtar, 1996). As a block to learning, pathological optimism prevents an individual from accounting for current problems, and this allows him or her to justify pushing the resolution of these problems into the future. This may sound like simple procrastination, putting unpleasant tasks off until some later date, but pathological optimism goes a step further by believing the problem will resolve itself at some future date.

In the case of Lay and Skilling, pathological optimism allowed the executives to put off dealing with real problems facing the company. These problems included a chronic failure to generate enough revenue to sustain the company. Optimism may be necessary for sustaining social interaction, as Freud once observed, but it is not always the most helpful attitude in the face of a crumbling business model (see Peterson, 2000). In the end, optimism tends to create a sense of invulnerability and leads the organization to overlook potential threats.

THE DESTRUCTIVE SIDE OF RANK-BASED PERFORMANCE SYSTEMS

Of all the highly publicized practices that contributed to the downfall of Enron, one of the most lauded and most imitated management practices involved the performance review committee, which ranked employees and rewarded those who were perceived to be top performers. In rank-based performance systems, rank and seniority in the company no longer matter; employees could earn as much as 80% of total compensation, both directly and indirectly, through high rankings by the committee so that junior-level employees could make substantially more than senior-level managers. In fact, the system determined not only the top performers, but also the bottom performers, providing that the bottom 10% of performers each year would be fired.

The rank-based performance system adopted by Enron appeals to our belief in merit and fairness. In practice, however, all compensation systems become complicated by the nature of managerial work. As operational tasks shift from routine to novel, measurement of success becomes more difficult. For instance, the requirements of certain high-level managers at large companies are significantly complicated, making "objective" performance difficult to measure. Purely performance-based models, like a rank-based performance system, encourage taking big risks, which generates an all-or-nothing mentality among employees. Taking risks may have promised big payoffs for individuals, but these risks ultimately put the company at significant risk. Enron had little incentive to manage these risks. After all, it was the big risks that led to success, at least in the short term. Because the company benefited so handsomely from the risks, Enron's compliance and oversight often looked the other way when problems arose.

The rank system is known in the industry as "stack ranking" (Cohan, 2012) and is commonly known among employees as "rank and yank" because it forces employees into a normalized curve—ranking employees and then firing, or yanking, the bottom 10%. What is humbling about the process of ranking employees is that it many cases it creates a culture of fear, competition, and information withholding. It creates an environment in which individuals fear being among the bottom 10% of employees so they often strive to stay out of the bottom rather than shooting for the top. Employees also become so competitive that they avoid working with top performers in order to avoid helping others get in the top 10% at the risk of limiting their own chances. Finally, the system tends to stifle learning because employees are incentivized for withholding information.

Rank-based performance systems were lauded in the book *The War for Talent* published in 2001 and written by one of Skilling's former co-workers at McKinsey (Michaels, Handfield-Jones, & Axelrod, 2001). The book even recognized Enron's compensation method. The idea behind the stack ranking system became popular among business leaders because it seemed to reward performance rather than position. General Electric was one of the first companies to experiment with the rank-and-yank system under the leadership of then-CEO Jack Welsh but has since abandoned the rank-based performance method. Other companies, like Microsoft, continue to rely on a rank-based performance system, but its destructive effects appear to outweigh the benefits. Some have even suggested that the decline in Microsoft relative to its competitors is directly linked to the destructive culture that emerges when a company adopts a rank-based performance system (Eichenwald, 2012b).

Over time, organizations that emphasize pure performance overshadow learning, and executives become preoccupied with maintaining their current performance levels. Other organizations have devised ways to maintain the learning–performance balance. General Electric continues to pioneer innovative human resource practices. Unlike Enron, General Electric realized early on that performance must be aligned with a strong value of learning. The application of a rigid performance management system must align with a rigorous emphasis on learning. That is the conclusion drawn by Ron Ashkenas, senior partner at Schaffer Consulting. Ron has worked with a host of companies, including General Electric, to devise performance management systems that are more holistic and emphasize employee development and change along with bottom-line performance. The rank-based performance management systems have proved so difficult to administer that many organizations have abandoned the bell curve mentality altogether, despite some of its underlying merits.

CONTRARIAN THINKING: THE CASE AGAINST OPTIMISM

There is a remedy to the kind of thinking that prevailed in Enron and other similar companies. The remedy is contrarian thinking. Every business school student understands that to make money in the stock market requires buying at a low price in anticipation that the price will increase. The person will then sell the stock at a later date for a profit. Short sellers take this logic and turn it on its head. Short sellers sell high and buy low. That is to say, a short selling strategy requires that you sell a company's stock, in the hope that its price will fall, so that later you can buy the stock back at a lower price. Short sellers study companies that they believe will experience discontinuity in the foreseeable future. Short sellers hold an air of mystery because they often foresee breakdown before others do. Lurking within this world of short sellers is an extraordinary example of learning.

Jim Chanos, head of the investment firm Kynikos Associates, is as close as it comes to a master of contrarian thinking. It's not surprising that his firm's name, Kynikos, is translated as "the cynic." He learned the tricks of short sales while working for a small investment firm in Ohio. He followed a company called Baldwin-United. Baldwin-United had developed a unique insurance product that took advantage of a tax loophole. The company's head, a man by the name of Morley Thompson, projected such confidence in his new insurance product that he promised to reinvent the insurance industry. In 1982, most investment companies believed in the Baldwin-United strategy and encouraged their clients to purchase the company's stock. Chanos saw something different. He saw a company threatened by tax reform laws (see Staley, 1996).

Chanos relied on a complicated financial analysis to uncover fraud and deception. He created a detailed cash flow analysis to identify how the company made its money. His review of Baldwin-United's financial data revealed a complex set of relationships among the various Baldwin-United subsidiaries. Even more suspicious, he could not easily understand something important about Baldwin-United's business model: He failed to grasp how the company made money. He concluded that the company was not making any money, despite the fact that it was reporting regular earnings. It turns out he was correct. Baldwin-United announced it could not make a loan payment and declared bankruptcy. Chanos's career as one of the world's most successful short sellers had begun.

Short sellers reveal important lessons about learning in organizations. One lesson is that learning often requires attention to detail, diligence, and dogmatic pursuit to unravel a mystery. The pursuit of learning reveals new insights, or new ways of looking at a problem or organization. Short sellers are known for going to extremes to uncover threats to continuity and learning. Short sellers might go as far as interviewing former employees to learn about company practices or might obtain satellite images of a company. One firm even paid dock workers to count and then report the number of shipping containers that arrived at a dock to track its competitor's activity in the emerging market.

Short sellers help improve transparency, which is essential for learning. Companies like Enron rely on the inflated value of their stock price and the resulting shareholder equity to finance new acquisitions. Despite earnings, one company we studied showed negative cash flows year after year due to expensive acquisitions. In addition, the acquisitions themselves seemed strange because the company placed an irregularly high value on "good will." After a strong earnings report and subsequent run up in the stock price, officers of the company often sold large quantities of stock. Compensation practices favored short-term or simplistic outcomes. Other factors indicated the company was in real trouble. The company came under investigation by the Securities and Exchange Commission, and the company's external auditors began to distance themselves from the company in audits.

We can learn something else from observing the short sellers. Short sellers create an important counterbalance to corporate optimism. They serve as devil's advocate to the ambitiously optimistic corporations. They tend to flush out deceptive, inflated, or overvalued assets that put companies and markets at risk. Short sellers offer a contrarian view to the optimistic, often overly optimistic, outlook of corporate culture. Short sellers help expose dysfunctional optimism brought about by companies like Enron that utilized aggressive accounting procedures, lacked standards, and relied on poor internal audit controls to avoid detection. Even accounting practices that must be explained in great detail or use of accounting practices that must continually be defended provide warning signs to short sellers.

Short selling remains a controversial practice among those in the investment community. Since the practice was first recorded in the 1600s during the tulip bulb bubble, short sellers have been the target of negative publicity. Lawsuits by companies that have landed in the crosshairs of short sellers have ensued. The primary complaint waged against short sellers is that they conspire among themselves to bring down even healthy, profitable companies, ruining shareholder value.

Short sellers expose overly confident, overly optimistic, and sometimes fraudulent companies. Increasingly, mainstream analysts show reluctance to issue negative reports on companies, threatening transparency. The ratings agencies missed the risk in subprime mortgages that ignited and fueled the financial meltdown in 2008 and missed the European debt crisis that followed in 2011 (see Moran, 2012). They seem weary of saying anything that might be considered negative about a company. Well-funded companies have seen fit to launch expensive lawsuits against those who issue negative analysis of them. In other cases, ratings agencies are paid directly by the firms themselves. Even more likely, companies will sanction analysts who report negative information or recommendations.

LESSONS FOR LEARNING IN ORGANIZATIONS

Enron and other corporate disasters teach us a lot about threats to learning. In some cases, the most significant threats aren't necessarily business related, but psychological. In the case of Enron, the threats were born from overconfidence in short-term achievements and pathological optimism. The self-congratulatory style led to justification of adopting management strategies that in turn led to limited short-term success, but also threatened the company in the long run. A list of the lessons learned from these disasters might include the following:

- Complex accounting practices such as earnings management can legitimately be used to manage seasonal volatility in income, but these same practices can be used to cover up poor long-term performance.
- Taking excessive risks can result in short-term success, but the risks are just as likely to lead to medium- and long-term failure.
- Early and extreme successes often blind leaders to vulnerability and lead them to believe in a false causality: that their leadership and management practices led to success when in fact it was simply market forces at work.
- Early successes and the unrealistic expectations that follow often result in setting and pursuing unrealistic and overly ambitious goals.
- Compensation systems that reward the short-term performance of individuals often carry unintended consequences for the larger organization.
- A culture built on short-term performance, deceptive accounting practices, and mistrust cannot be sustained in a competitive business environment.
- Overly optimistic projections about future growth and confidence in one's management practices can lead to justification of deceptive and even illegal practices such as irresponsible management earnings practices.
- Poorly managed risk within the company is a threat to learning.
- Leaders may be unwilling or unable to adapt to changes in the external environment at the expense of learning, change, and growth.
- Leaders can easily become disengaged from the day-to-day operations of the organization (pie in the sky ideas).

CONCLUSION

This chapter has explored how certain common management practices such as earnings management and various performance management systems limit learning in organizations. Often executives adopt these management practices because they hold an uncompromising optimism in the success of their company and they falsely attribute their short-term success to these management practices. Certain accounting and financial practices allow organizations to maintain a public face of optimism and success, despite underlying problems with their business model. These processes limit learning, and they also expose the role of deception, both intentional and unintentional. Skeptics such as short sellers are described as making sure that learning occurs and offsetting some of the underlying threats to learning.

CHAPTER 7

Goal Setting as an Unlikely Threat to Learning

GOAL FEVER

In the space race to reach the moon, the United States set a goal to put a person on the moon and to bring the person back. Achieving the goal was assigned to the National Aeronautics and Space Administration (NASA). The goal was achieved, but not without unintended consequences. In an effort to meet the goal, safety precautions were overlooked, technology contingencies were not well thought out, and alternative exit strategies were ignored. Two astronauts died as a capsule exploded in a test flight when, due to time constraints, faulty wiring was not inspected. Despite the early successes of the Apollo program and the ultimate success in reaching the goal, this accident threatened the entire system by exposing potential unintended outcomes that might arise during the pursuit of the goal of reaching the moon.

Just days after the tragic accident, flight control commander Gene Kranz (2000) presented his analysis of what went wrong. He concluded that NASA had become a victim of "goal fever." Never again, he asserted, would the Apollo program put the safety of its people at the mercy of achieving the goal. The story of goal fever at NASA provides an opportunity to consider the often-overlooked consequences of goals, goal setting, and the process of goal pursuit.

Goal setting remains an influential theory in organizational behavior (Miner, 2003) and maintains an almost cult-like status among practicing managers. Despite its popularity as a management practice, there is growing concern that under some circumstances goal setting can go awry, resulting in unintended consequences and even destructive outcomes. Research has shown that under many conditions, setting goals improves performance over simply urging individuals to do their best (see Locke & Latham, 1990). Despite the benefit of goals and goal setting, there is growing concern that goals may also contain a darker side, but calls to reconsider goal setting have gained little traction among academics because the research on goal setting is believed to hold overwhelming support in research. However, recent debates among practice-based journals provide insights into how learning can be threatened when organizations emphasize goal setting at the expense of learning (Kayes, 2005; Latham & Locke, 2006; Locke & Latham, 2009; Ordonez, Schweitzer, Galinsky, & Bazerman, 2009a,b).

Although the processes that facilitate effective goal setting are well understood, the processes by which goal setting breaks down and the negative consequences emerge remain largely unaddressed. Of the four types of vulnerability offered by Wilensky and outlined earlier in the book, vulnerability to goals is the least understood. Since the processes that lead to breakdown often differ from the processes that lead to success (Mohr, 1982), both theory and practice are left without a coherent model of how goal setting threatens learning. Before further discussing the negative consequences of goal setting, two more cases illustrate the point.

Goal Fever in the Montparnasse Train Derailment

Nineteen years of experience engineering a train failed Guillaume-Marie Pellerin. A train of 12 cars, including eight passenger cars carrying 131 passengers, had left Granville at 8:45 in the morning, headed for Paris. By 3:55 that afternoon, Pellerin noticed the train he was driving was running 10 minutes late. It would not arrive on schedule, he thought, so he decided to make up for lost time.

He conducted a train equipped with the latest technology, the Westinghouse quick action automatic brakes. The new technology relied on hydraulics rather than friction to stop the train. As the train approached the station, Pellerin applied the Westinghouse brake, but the train was running too fast. In fact, regulations prohibited Pellerin from applying the new braking system once he had entered the train station because the brakes had not been fully tested and were thought to be unreliable at high speeds. The air braking system was not designed to stop a train traveling as fast as the 40 to 60 kilometers per hour that Pellerin was traveling. The hydraulic brake failed. By now, the train was racing through the station. Pellerin applied the standard friction brake, but it was too late.

A second train engineer, Albert Mariette, provided no help. As the train approached the station, he was unaware of the dire situation that Pellerin had created. The train raced through the station as Mariette sat in the back of the train finishing up the paperwork. Finishing the paperwork would avoid any further delay in the schedule, he thought. The runaway engine and its 12 attached cars plowed through the bumper and then crashed through the west wall of the station. The locomotive didn't stop until it had fallen 30 feet onto the street below, on the Place de Rennes. The rest of the train, remarkably, remained relatively intact. Everyone on the train survived, including the two conductors, Monsieurs Pellerin and Mariette. Unfortunately, a woman selling newspapers on the Place de Rennes was killed by falling stones. The train did, however, arrive at the station by 4:00 p.m., exactly as the Monsieurs had planned!

Pellerin testified to the accident investigation committee that the train crash resulted from the failure of the Westinghouse brake. But because engaging the Westinghouse brake, rather than the traditional braking method, was prohibited once the train breached the station, the investigating committee concluded that the accident was caused by Pellerin's use of excessive speed as he tried to make up for lost time (Richou, 1895; see also Laurendon & Laurendon, 1997).

A photograph of the disaster captured by Levy and Sons now hangs in the Musée d'Orsay in Paris. It depicts the train locomotive conducted by Pellerin with its nose face down on the Place de Rennes. The derailment of the Granville to Paris train tells us something about learning in organizations. Many factors contributed to the Montparnasse train derailment of 1895: a late train, a conductor inexperienced in applying the brakes at high speed, an untested technology, unfinished paperwork, growing pressures to meet scheduled arrival times, and the temptation to bend the rules in order to meet a deadline. Together these factors offer clues on why learning broke down for Pellerin and Mariette.

The train derailment at Montparnasse helps to frame our understanding of how people in organizations learn from experience and what consequences ensue when learning breaks down. At its heart, learning involves gathering and processing knowledge to serve in solving problems, but for the conductors on the Granville to Montparnasse train, learning proved elusive. Learning broke down as events quickly moved from routine procedures to novel situations. The shift from routine to novel required Pellerin and Mariette to quickly learn. In the end, the demands of learning and the associated integration of thoughts, feelings, and actions proved overwhelming. Pellerin achieved his goal—the train arrived on time—but the unintended consequence of this achievement proved more harmful than failure to meet the deadline.

Goal Fever and the Efficiency of Emergency Medicine

Imagine that you have an unfortunate injury that requires that you be rushed to the emergency room of a regional hospital. When you arrive, you are put into a queue of other patients and are told to wait in the waiting room until your name is called. After waiting for three and a half hours, your name is finally called. You are not ushered into the emergency room, however; instead, you are ushered into an inpatient hospital bed. Your injury remains undiagnosed and neglected. Several days later, a doctor visits your room and diagnoses your injury.

Imagine also that the decision to move you from the waiting room, and immediate emergency room care, to a hospital bed resulted not from the desire to care for your health, but to meet a requirement that all patients be moved through the emergency care system within four hours. A concern that the goal-setting process may facilitate undesirable outcomes has grown in emergency care medicine (Weber, Mason, Carter, & Hew, 2011). Hardern (2012) described the destructive pursuit of goals to analyze the impact of the "4-h" goal of caring for patients and moving them out of the emergency room within four hours of arrival. He argued that within the British health system, the 4-h goal has led to more timely care, but lower quality of care. There is support for his hypothesis from a study conducted by Weber et al. (2011). Hardern equated the 4-h goal to medicine that may be helpful on the surface, but that carries undesirable side effects.

The NASA Apollo program, the train derailment at Montparnasse, and the 4-h emergency room goal provide organizational examples of a growing concern with goal setting and pursuit among management and organization scholars: that under certain conditions, goal setting can have detrimental and even disastrous effects on organizational learning and that goals often carry unintended consequences that can lead to harm. Nor are these concerns isolated to a few organizations that may have misread or misapplied goal setting. A growing body of systematic research may confirm some of this concern.

EMPIRICAL RESEARCH ON THE EFFECTS OF GOALS

Ayelet Fishbach studied how individuals regulate their own behavior in various situations. Goals play an important part in self-regulation because they serve to direct a person to a future desired state (Fishbach & Choi, 2012). Fishbach argued that pursuing a goal carries two distinct but often related benefits. First, pursuing a goal creates a positive experience. The activity itself has intrinsic value. Riding a roller coaster, spending time with friends, or playing on a softball league—all of these activities hold intrinsic value; the experience itself is worthwhile, regardless of the outcome. Pursuit of goals carries an instrumental benefit as well. Instrumental benefits are outcomes of the experience. In organizations, goals are set to improve performance, achieve sales targets, improve revenue, and for a host of other desired outcomes. On a personal level, a person may set a goal to lose weight, finish a triathlon, make more money, or save for a new car. Of course, most activities have both an instrumental and experiential benefit. For example, spending time with friends can become instrumental if it is done in order to build a professional network or develop business. Professional baseball players probably enjoy playing baseball, but there are instrumental goals as well associated with the job.

Fishbach wanted to understand if setting goals improved goal achievement. She uncovered a fundamental problem with the goal-setting process, something that management scholars have suspected for years but had not been able to verify directly in a scientific manner. In certain circumstances, setting goals undermines the pursuit of goals. One conclusion that Fishbach came to was that while an instrumental goal promotes the intention to pursue a goal, it decreases the effort put forth in pursuing the goal. She came to this conclusion after conducting four tests at or near the University of Chicago in which individuals set and pursued goals in four areas: (1) origami, the Japanese art of paper folding; (2) exercise at a gym; (3) flossing teeth; and (4) yoga. Although these tasks are quite different, she believed that each had both an experiential (intrinsic) as well as instrumental (extrinsic) goal. Yoga, for example, both felt good and created social bonds (intrinsic) and improved strength, flexibility, and overall mental health (extrinsic). In each of the four areas, she compared individuals who were prompted to set intrinsic goals with those who were prompted to set extrinsic goals. She found that when individuals were prompted to focus on extrinsic goals, their intention to engage in the activity increased, but the time they spent in the activity actually decreased! In other words, the individuals spent more time planning to pursue the goal, but less time working on pursuing the goal. Those in the exercise study, for example, who thought about instrumental outcomes such as losing weight had higher intentions to work out, but actually worked out less than those who were prompted to focus on intrinsic goals like stretching and running on the treadmill.

Even more interesting, Fishbach found that the intention didn't even have to be explicit for this phenomenon to occur. Individuals' intentions are largely out of their awareness, as she discovered in her test of yoga participants. In the yoga test, she divided a yoga class into two groups. In one group, she provided a copy of the cover of a yoga magazine along with the initial study survey. The cover depicted only a smiling woman engaging in yoga. The second group was provided with a cover that pictured the same woman, but also had short phrases that promoted the benefits of yoga, including "peak performance, calm, energy, and brainpower." Participants with only the picture spent more time on yoga, whereas participants exposed to the instrumental benefits spent more time on intention to engage in yoga, but less time on yoga itself. Introducing the extrinsic goal, it seems, actually decreased participation in the activity.

These studies have implications for learning in organizations. When people in organizations focus on achieving organizational-level goals, the task is rendered less valuable and people actually expend less effort, time, and resources to achieving the task. When the learning process is intrinsic, such as developing new insights, engaging in enjoyable conversation, or improving performance, people are more likely to engage in the process and learn. In chapter 6, we explored why this insight into learning often renders many compensation and reward systems in organizations ineffective and in some cases dysfunctional: Instrumental goals such as incentives and pay for performance may actually decrease time spent pursuing goals but increase time discussing the achievement of goals. Thus, extrinsic learning goals may decrease learning or at a minimum decrease the potential for learning. One conclusion that can be drawn is that during preparation for an activity, people should focus on the outcome, but once they actually start engaging in the pursuit of the goal, they should adjust their focus to the task itself and its intrinsic qualities.

GOAL PURSUIT AS THE CAUSE OF BREAKDOWN

Fishbach's research suggests that goal setting may actually decrease the effort put into a task. Fischbach's research confirms a growing concern with the unintended consequences of goal setting.

One way that goal pursuit can fuel the breakdown of learning is related to ethics. Schweitzer, Ordonez, and Douma (2004) found that the presence of individual goals motivates people to engage in unethical decision making. Individuals who set high and specific goals were more likely to lie about their performance than those who had no goals or very general goals. The researchers created three groups. The researchers told one group to "do your best" and then gave participants $10. The researchers gave the second group an exact goal, to "create nine words," and then gave them a flat $10 for participation. The researchers told the third group that their goal was to create nine words. The researchers handed this group an envelope containing $14 and told the participants to keep $2 each time they met their goal. The latter two groups were more likely to overstate actual performance; individuals simply told to do their best were less likely to exaggerate performance. In addition, those who were closest to achieving their goals were more likely to overstate performance than those far from achieving their goals. In all, about 30% of participants with reward-based goals overstated their performance.

A second form of breakdown of learning that emerges from goal pursuit relates to increased risk taking, as demonstrated by a study conducted by Knight, Durham, and Locke (2001). Greater risk taking by organizations may result in more favorable outcomes, but the benefits of taking greater risks in high-reliability organizations may be offset by the potential for disastrous consequences. Further, extensive research has revealed that escalation of commitment to an existing course of action at the individual, group, and organizational level may make abandoning a goal difficult or impossible. Evidence from several case studies builds a convincing argument that once a goal is set, organizations have difficulty abandoning it, even when faced with consequences such as death and financial disaster (Ross & Staw, 1993).

Earley, Connolly, and Ekegren (1989) identified yet a third way that goal pursuit can lead to breakdown. Their study showed that goal setting limited problem-solving activity and performance during a comprehensive and ill-defined task. They asked participants to try to pick stock prices for 100 imaginary firms. Researchers provided only a limited amount of information to the participants. Participants were assigned to two groups. The researchers told the first group to meet a specific difficult goal: to guess the stock price within $10 of the actual stock price. In contrast, researchers told the second group to "do your best." As evidence of the difficulty of the task, in pretests individuals estimated correctly only about 15% of the time. Participants who had high and specific goals were less successful than those who were simply trying to do their best. The researchers became so baffled that they re-ran the experiment three more times, and the same results emerged each time.

The researchers also found that the group with specific goals tried more and different strategies to achieve their goal. The researchers intentionally designed the task so that several different strategies might produce correct or near-correct responses. The different strategies that could have produced success for the participants were so numerous, in fact, that trying different strategies became counterproductive. Even though it appeared the group was learning, after all they were trying different strategies, the task was so complicated, simply trying new strategies resulted in counterproductive results. What was needed was indepth learning and analysis, not attempts at pattern matching.

The researchers concluded their analysis by suggesting three levels of task and goal achievement. The first level focuses on the content of the task itself. When performance can be improved by increasing effort and energy, then goal setting works well. Examples would be situations that require manual work or simple production. The second level consists of a task that requires specific strategies to complete. Here, setting a specific and difficult goal works best because once a single best strategy is identified, it tends to work well all the time. At the third level, however, goal setting goes awry. Successful performance at this third level requires continued learning and development of new strategies. Successful performance cannot be achieved from simple trial and error but only through detailed learning. The study suggested that when a task can be achieved by many possible solutions, goal setting actually creates new problems and limits effectiveness. They concluded that goal setting is better suited to solutions in which quantity, rather than quality, of output is best. This finding suggests that goal setting can create vulnerabilities when the task itself is complex, time bound, and difficult.

Sitkin, See, Miller, Lawless, and Carton (2011), writing from the perspective of organizational strategy, revealed yet another source of vulnerability to breakdown of learning that emerges during goal pursuit. They argued that stretch goals have a negative impact on learning, especially among organizations whose assessment of the complexity of the task is insufficient to successfully execute the goal.

Perhaps the most incendiary view of goals is presented in my 2006 book on the process of destructive goal pursuit. In this conceptualization, destructive goal pursuit arises when a leader sets a single, narrow goal, measured by a short-term outcome that results in a situation in which the goal becomes difficult to abandon, despite evidence that it cannot be achieved. Several exogenous and endogenous variables fuel this process, including public expectation that the goal

Table 7.1. VARIABLES AND OUTCOMES ASSOCIATED WITH DESTRUCTIVE
GOAL PURSUIT

Category	Factor
Latent beliefs	• The idealization of a future state • Failure to identify unintended consequences • Pursuit that is justified by the goal itself and not other logic • The feeling that achieving the goal is destiny
Observable factors	• A narrowly defined goal (focuses on "relevant" task characteristics but devalues other characteristics) • A prevailing public expectation that achieving the goal is imminent • Face-saving behavior displayed by the team or individual
Underlying causes	• Identity maintenance • Belief confirmation • Cohesion • Goal-setting determination/persistence • Redemption, just reward, payoff • Performance versus learning orientation • Self-image preservation
Outcomes	• Reluctance to abandon goal, even in the face of disconfirming evidence • Unethical decisions • Excessive risk-taking • Inability to accomplish goal • Ignoring of unintended consequences • Breakdown of learning
Task characteristics	• Complexity • Duration • Unknown cause-and-effect relationship • Politics and interpretation of goals • Ill-structured task

will be achieved, association of the goal with destiny, face-saving behavior, an overly romanticized or optimistic vision of expected outcomes, and goal-related justification for continued pursuit of the goal. These variables result in a situation in which the normally helpful processes of goal setting and pursuit lead to unintended, even disastrous consequences (e.g., Turner, 1976). Table 7.1 outlines variables, explanations, and outcomes associated with destructive goal pursuit.

Critiques of This View

Goal-setting advocates have offered three types of responses to the preceding findings. First, they have offered a set of boundary conditions under which goal setting is said to work (Latham & Locke, 2006). Among their comments were that goal setters need to have the knowledge, skills, and motivation to complete the task, and goal conflict within an individual or a group may make achieving any specific goal difficult or lead to the perception of goal setting as a threat rather than a challenge. A second response attempted to expand the definition of what constitutes goal setting to activities typically associated with learning (Seijts et al., 2004). To expand into this territory, goal-setting theorists have turned to goal orientation theory, which distinguishes between performance goals and learning goals. By expanding the definition, the theorists respond to critics of goals by expanding the definition of goal setting and indicating that breakdown of goals may happen in scenarios in which there are activities not typically associated with goals. The third response, rather than focusing on the theoretical grounding of goal-setting theory, redirected attention to the empirical research that points to the positive outcomes of goal setting (Miner, 2002). This third response, essentially, ignores the negative potential of goals because the positive outcomes can outweigh the negative outcomes.

Although the attempts to set boundary conditions, expand definitions, and redirect attention provide attractive theoretical and rhetorical tools, they do little to respond to two underlying issues with goal setting. First, as mentioned, there is a substantial and growing research base that reveals important unintended consequences to goal setting, which these responses fail to address. In this regard, attempts to focus simply on the positive outcomes of goal setting have the feel of selective attention, in which positive outcomes are offered but unintended consequences are explained away or overlooked altogether. Second, the central challenge to goal-setting theory is that the underlying theory lacks theoretical coherence (see Miner, 2002); because it has been developed inductively over the course of 30 years, the theory has undergone a good bit of patching and re-definition. Although this approach is expected in any theory that has received such an impressive amount of attention, the result is a failure to answer important questions and to address limitations in the goal-setting process.

A MORE COMPREHENSIVE MODEL FOR
GOAL SETTING AND PURSUIT

An important question remains unanswered: What happens if the conditions needed to achieve the vision begin to erode? What if the goal needs to be revised based on new information or changes in the environment? What if the goal needs to be abandoned altogether? Destructive goal pursuit answers this question and can be summarized as follows: The more a leader identifies with a future, as yet unachieved, goal, or vision, the more likely the leader will be dependent on that goal for his or her identity. In addition, as the leader devotes resources to achieving that goal or vision, the less likely he or she will be to abandon the goal or vision, even in the face of contradictory information.

To address the limitations of goal setting, I propose a comprehensive model that recognizes the influence of factors such as task characteristics, organizational culture, and exogenous factors (Figure 7.1). This model considers both

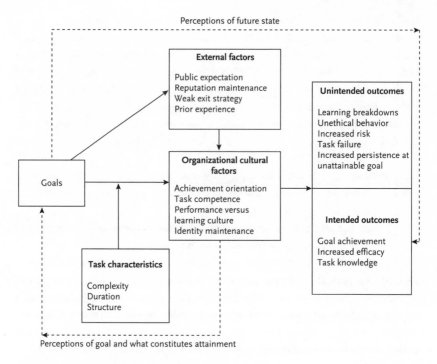

Figure 7.1:
An integrated model of the goal setting and pursuit process.

the intended and unintended consequences of goal setting and pursuit. Specific measurable goals result in improved goal achievement, task knowledge, and task efficacy, as consistent with goal-setting theory. The model also considers the unintended consequences that may result: increased risk, unethical behavior, and breakdown of learning.

Endogenous variables, which we equate with an organizational culture of goal setting, focus on achievement orientation, task competence, a performance versus learning culture, and identity maintenance to mediate the relationship between goals and outcomes. Learning orientation is an important aspect of culture (see March, 1991), and identity maintenance is expected to both increase goal achievement but also increase risk and continued pursuit of goals (Kayes, 2005). The model suggests that factors in organizational culture moderate the relationship between goals and goal achievement, resulting in both intended and unintended consequences.

Exogenous pressures influence goal achievement indirectly and organizational culture directly. When an organization experiences outside pressure, it may be more likely to limit critical thinking and be less likely to consider multiple strategies for success, and therefore be less likely to abandon its goals. Research from finance and accounting, for example, has found that organizations face increased pressure to "manage" their results for outside observers such as analysts and rating agencies (Mulford & Comiskey, 2002). For example, publicly held companies often offer "guidance" on quarterly earnings, and achieving these targets is sometimes linked to internal goals and rewards. The goals that are established set expectations for external stakeholders that then in turn influence the internal culture of goal performance. The relationship among goals, external image, and internal culture has been seen in at least one investigation into earnings manipulation and so-called "earnings management" (see, for example, Rudman, Parker, Oh, & Kramer, 2006). Similarly, within the government sector, the National Security Agency (NSA), the collection and assessment arm of the U.S. intelligence community, sent out bids to build a next-generation software package that would surf through trillions of bits of data collected by the agency. The goal was to identify patterns that could pinpoint terrorist activity. The goal appeared noble, but a few years into the project, it emerged as undoable as the project incurred extensive cost overruns. By the time NSA finally scrapped the "Trailblazer" project, the tab was estimated at $1.7 billion for a software package that never went into operation (Gorman, 2006). Finally, prior experience considers successes and failures within a particular industry setting (Audia, Locke, & Smith, 2000). For this reason, the model proposes that exogenous factors have a direct impact on how the organization perceives the goal and its importance.

It is well established from both research and theory that task characteristics play an important role in the success of task outcomes. Task characteristics are defined along two dimensions. First, task complexity is concerned with the number of variables essential for completing the task as well as the changes in those variables (Campbell, 1988). The second related consideration is the task structure, whether the task is ill structured or well structured. A well-structured task has a finite number of interpretations, variables, and outcomes. An ill-structured task includes multiple variables, many of which may be unknown or unaccounted for, and has multiple outcomes, few of which will be achieved. Setting specific measurable goals is thought to be more effective when tasks are well structured and hold little complexity because goal setting focuses individuals on those task characteristics that are most relevant to goal achievement. Third, task duration, whether the task is conceptualized as a short- or long-term process, will also have an impact (Campbell, 1988). The model, therefore, considers that task characteristics moderate the relationship between specific measurable goals and goal achievement.

The proposed model provides an integrative framework for capturing both the intended and unintended consequences of goals, goal setting, and goal pursuit. Further, when pursuing goals, organizations often re-frame goals based on current interpretations, as the goals shape interpretations of how future events will unfold. As an interpretive framework, the model offers a guide for future research to consider specific cases of goal setting and its consequences. Experimental designs that involve goals as experimental treatments could offer additional insights into what factors may influence overpursuit of goals and goal justification. Cross-sectional correlational studies could also offer insight to determine, for example, under which conditions performance versus learning goals are more likely to lead to unproductive goal setting and which personality factors are more likely to lead to destructive goal pursuit. Other research might investigate the role played by various incentives and social supports. In particular, cross-sectional correlational studies would be valuable to generate hypotheses about which factors may be most important to isolate for further study.

DESTRUCTIVE GOAL PURSUIT AND ITS RELATION TO OTHER THEORIES

In organizations, the negative impact of goals can increase because the destructive pursuit of goals involves not just the leader, but also a group of committed followers. The followers may be attached to the leader because he or she carries formal authority, or the followers may be attached to the leader because of his or her compelling vision. Either way, the community of followers becomes dependent on the leader for their own identity.

The theoretical underpinnings of destructive goal pursuit emerge from learning theory, but are linked to leadership studies and the psychology of organizations. It is also linked to existing explanations as to why leaders and their followers might cling to a vision, despite mounting evidence that it cannot be attained. Although the notion that goals and vision can themselves be destructive is relatively underdeveloped, there are several related concepts that reveal some of the underlying mechanisms of destructive goal pursuit.

Social-Identity Theory

Social identity provides a potent explanation for the underlying forces of destructive goal pursuit in organizations and teams. Social identity theory suggests that individual identity is tied to belonging to or being associated with a group. Being part of a group involves two dimensions. First, you must identify with an "in-group" to which you see yourself belonging. Second, you must distinguish yourself from an "out-group" from which you see yourself as distinct. In other words, it is not enough to identify with a particular group; you must also see yourself as distinct from other groups. The need to identify with a group is a strong social force. Many motivation theorists believe that being affiliated with a group—feeling a positive sense of belonging and working toward maintaining relationships within the group—is one of the strongest behavioral forces.

Goals represent a desired future state, and goal setting offers a pathway to create that desired state. As such, goal setting represents a distinct process of identity construction, because individuals use goals as a basis of identity or set goals to reinforce a desired identity. From the perspective of learning, a fundamental problem with goal setting and task performance is that it views a goal as a fixed entity, rather than something that is negotiated as time goes by. It is not the goals specifically that motivate the individual employees as much as it is their own individual view of the future formed as a result of these goals. Because a future desired goal can serve as the group's identity, the goal becomes as difficult to abandon as the group's identity.

Escalation of Commitment

The social identity perspective on goals shares characteristics with escalation of commitment (Staw, 1981), which refers to the processes by which individuals, groups, and organizations contribute energy and resources to a failing course of action. In this line of thinking, agents become entrapped by their persistence toward achieving certain predefined goals. Staw suggested that individuals often commit to a course of action too quickly and continue to pursue it far beyond the point of receiving any rational benefit. The goal-setting process often helps to commit assignees to this course of action early on in the process. Fear of failure in the face of relevant constituencies and the breakdown of rational processes in the face of political forces are also expected to escalate commitment (Clegg et al., 2006). Organizations may engage in goal setting and establish goals as a way to build institutional legitimacy, which in turn creates incentives for interpreting outcomes as consistent with such goals (Gioia & Thomas, 1996).

The escalation of commitment perspective provides a retrospective explanation for present action. It suggests that current decisions are driven by past actions. Failure in past decision making in particular will entice individuals, groups, and organizations to make greater investments in a particular courses of action. Other interpretations of the escalation of commitment approach have begun to surface. Escalation may occur because an action is related to project timelines, in which individuals tend to increase commitment as a project nears completion (Garland & Conlon, 1998). Under this interpretation, escalation occurs because of commitment to completion, to getting a project done, rather than to prior decisions. The paradox of success approach (Audia et al., 2000) also tries to relate escalation of commitment to factors other than past success. In a series of laboratory studies, as well as interpretation of industrial examples, a group of researchers identified that organizations will commit to a course of action based on past failures as well as successes. The thinking is that if an organization has failed previously, it is even more fixated on continuing to pursue a goal, so as not to fail again. The same logic holds up to organizations that have previously experienced success. Success fuels an organization's continued fixation on the goal. Whether the commitment is to past failures, successes, or the completion of a project itself, the escalation perspective suggests that commitment is consistent with the notion of destructive goal pursuit because it points to commitment to an existing course of action that is difficult to abandon, even in the face of disconfirming evidence.

Groupthink

Destructive goal pursuit is closely related to groupthink and may simply be a situation whereby group cohesion is formed around a future vision or goal of the future (see Burnette, Forsyth, & Pollack, 2011). The notion of destructive goal pursuit, then, adds a specific form of dysfunctional behavior to leadership nomenclature that occurs when a leader puts too much weight on the achievement of future goals. By focusing on future goals, individuals can make sense of future events in terms of future potential achievements or circumstances.

Self-Deception

In some cases, idealizing a future can lead to unrealistic expectations and results in disappointment. Research on self-deception provides a partial explanation for why goals lead to failure as well. Smith, Loewenstein, Jankovich, and Ubel (2009) found that patients with no hope of recovering from colostomy surgery adjusted better than those who had only temporary colostomies. The patients who experienced permanent life changes had higher scores on two dimensions of adjustment to illness, quality of life, and life satisfaction, than those who had only temporary life changes six months after surgery. The study has interesting implications for goals and goal setting because it suggests that people who take a long view are better able to adapt to change, whereas those who experience temporary setbacks actually take longer to adjust to change. A realistic assessment up front provides a better foundation for adjustment than learning bad news later. Coming to a slow realization that one cannot achieve a goal seems to be less adaptive in the long run.

One reason that goals may lead to detrimental effects in organizations is because goals serve as a mechanism for self-deception. Professors Michael Robinson and Carol Ryff (1999) reviewed the psychological research on self-deception and found that self-deception increased during two situations. The first is when leaders lack concrete information. For example, when leaders are trying to decide which candidate to hire, they might engage in self-deception to "fill in the blanks" about a potential candidate's qualifications. Second, self-deception increases when leaders are highly motivated to deceive. One study showed that leaders were more likely to lie when the incentive was high; for example, leaders would be more likely to engage in self-deception about performance if they expected to receive some payment for a certain level of performance. The series of studies by Robinson and Ryff offers some important lessons about self-deception and goals. As expected, self-deception is more likely to occur in the face of an uncertain future. The more data available, the less likely self-deception will occur. The research also revealed that people tend to be more optimistic about their performance in the future than past performance warrants. Finally, people feel that they will have greater control over future events than they did over past events. For example, participants in the study reported that they expected higher degrees of happiness, life satisfaction, and self-esteem in the future, relative to their past and current states.

These studies imply that leaders carry more confidence in their future prospects than in past performance. There is a connection to goals, goal pursuit, and self-deception. Goals may serve as a form of self-deception because they decrease uncertainty about the future, cause leaders to overestimate competence, and create unwarranted optimism about the future. In other cases, leaders deceive followers by simply adapting the goals of the group to appear more persuasive. One study (Gray & Densten, 2007) of more than 2,000 business and academic leaders revealed some important relationships between self-deception and goals. The researchers found that self-deception was highly related to the degree to which a leader fostered goals, intellectual stimulation, and rewards among followers. One of the strongest relationships, however, was between self-deception and the use of goals. Leaders tried to gain credibility by appearing to promote team goals and encourage teamwork. This tactic had the effect of building team cohesion and commitment to the team's goals; however, the leaders did not necessarily promote the achievement of the goal itself, nor did they foster expectations of high performance.

But there is another, perhaps more disturbing finding from this study. Leaders actually believed they would achieve the goal even though they put little effort into achieving it. The leaders focused on building cohesion and gaining loyalty among followers but ignored building behaviors that might actually lead to achieving the goal. In the study, building a shared sense of goals fostered cohesion and loyalty, just as expected, but building a shared goal didn't actually facilitate goal achievement. It seems that setting goals does not necessarily focus leaders on actually achieving the goals. In fact, it seems that many leaders may be inclined to foster the value of goal setting, but display few behaviors that facilitate goal achievement. This makes sense. For many, leading involves promoting a positive view of the future, but achieving that positive future is actually secondary to building loyalty. The leader appeals to the followers based on their emotions, their desired vision of the future, not necessarily the realization of that future.

CONCLUSION

Destructive goals serve as a hidden source of breakdown in organizations. The variety of applications suggests that the concept has strong currency for practicing managers and could serve as a framework to bridge theory and practice (Rynes, 2007). Destructive goal pursuit has been mentioned as one of the top explanations, along with groupthink and escalation of commitment, for disasters and mishaps, for example, in mountain climbing and adventure travel (Zook, 2011). The medical metaphor seems to have gained traction in discussions of goal setting, as Ordonez et al. (2009a) described goal setting as an overprescribed management technique that often leads to adverse consequences. The concept of side effects from goals has also appeared in discussions of self-management (De Oliveira, 2009; Wasmund & Newton, 2012).

This chapter has explained one important set of threats to learning in organizations. This framework offers an alternative interpretation of goal setting as a process of identity construction and maintenance. This provides a means to view goal setting as a holistic process that engenders unintended but often predictable consequences. This is the first step in understanding the underlying mechanisms of goal setting that lead organizations to create phrases like "goal fever" and cause researchers to explore how learning can erode under the compelling allure of goals.

CHAPTER 8
Experience and Decision Making

THE 2008 FINANCIAL MELTDOWN

During the most trying moments of the global financial meltdown of 2008, the head of a major investment bank struggled to make decisions that would ultimately impact the survival of his company. His decisions, by all accounts, failed. As his company slowly collapsed, the executive ignored information, distrusted his advisors, and ultimately stood by as his inaction fueled the collapse of Lehman Brothers. Just a month earlier, the U.S. Treasury had offered to broker a deal in which the executive would sell the company for $46 per share, but the company ignored this opportunity. Less than five months later, the stock was acquired for about $2 per share. Even with his personal fortune at stake, one of the most experienced decision makers in the world failed to take a course of action that could have saved the company. His personal fortune as head of the company, held in the form of his company's stock, evaporated, resulting in a personal loss of more than $1 billion (Sorkin, 2009; see also Paulson, 2010). Figure 8.1 shows the stock price of Lehman Brothers between January 2008 and September 2008. Figure 8.2 shows the stock price from August 1, 2008, until it filed for bankruptcy on September 15, 2008.

Not only did individual decision making break down, but so did the systematic, state-of-the-art organizational mechanisms designed to support effective (and avoid poor) decision making. The compensation system experienced breakdown even though Lehman had adopted one of the most progressive compensation systems available, designed to ensure that individual compensation was closely linked to both personal and firm performance. Training and education seemed to break down as well. The decision makers themselves were educated at the top universities and received continuing executive education by the best educators. Even decision making itself seemed to break down as Lehman had developed and implemented the latest decision-making tools and processes.

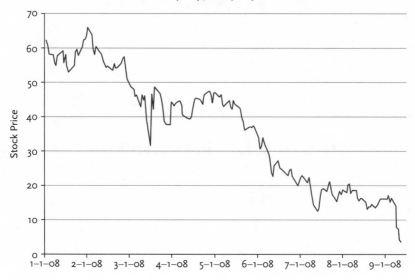

Figure 8.1:
The stock price of Lehman Brothers from January to September 2008.

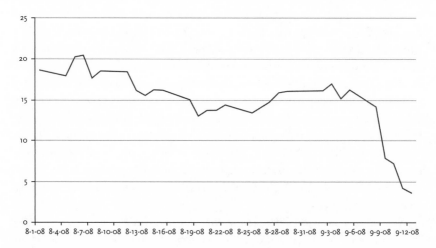

Figure 8.2:
Lehman stock prices from August 1, 2008, until it filed for chapter 11 bankruptcy on September 15, 2008.

The company had invested heavily to develop the most advanced and complex decision-making technology, hired the best analysts, and constantly updated the most timely and sophisticated mathematical models ever devised. Even strategic management principles experienced breakdown as Lehman's corporate strategy had been devised and revised by some of the most renowned business strategists in the world.

As experts continue to analyze the largest bankruptcy in history, many stand perplexed. How could an organization with the most advanced compensation systems, training, technology and advice break down so completely during a moment of crisis? Perhaps something beyond the systems themselves was at play. Perhaps the breakdown occurred due to the limits associated with the kinds of formal decision making practiced in most organizations.

The events reveal that rational decision making can pose a threat to learning. Five approaches to decision making are described: rational, economic-based behavioral, organizational-based behavioral, evidence-based, and experiential based. A process that integrates multiple forms of information and decision-making processes is proposed.

DECISION MAKING: A BRIEF OVERVIEW

Paul Nutt (2002) conducted an extensive review of decisions made in organizations. Studying nearly 500 decisions, his research revealed that, even under the best conditions, about half of the decisions made in organizations fail. Most decisions had about as much chance of working as simply flipping a coin!

Why do management efforts fail so often? According to Nutt, decisions fail for two main reasons. First, most decisions fail because most decisions of great consequence occur in the face of novelty. Novel experiences, as we have discussed, create problems of extreme complexity. In the face of novel experiences, an organization faces rules that have never before been faced. Actions, once taken, create unintended consequences that are so unpredictable that organizations seldom get it right the first time. Only with trial and error, adjustment, and reconsideration can most large-scale managerial decisions result in success. A second reason that most organizational decisions fail the first time is that the decision maker relies on simple linear responses to complex nonlinear problems.

Garvin and Roberto (2001) supported Nutt's explanation for why so many organizational decisions fail. They suggested that decisions fail because decision makers see decisions as one-time events, whereas they advocated for a concept of decision making that coincides with a process of continual learning. In order to make effective decisions, organizations need to continually respond and update in the face of initial failures and challenges.

If half of all organizational decisions end in failure, then the quality of the first decision may matter less than how the organization responds to setbacks that emerge after the first action is taken. Learning becomes more important than decision making as an organization finds ways to recover, respond, update, and coordinate in the face of initial and subsequent setbacks. When an experience is characterized by novelty and complexity, the key to successful decision making is the ability to respond to feedback, not reliance on the probability of a single event. What matters in making effective decisions is the ability of the organization to learn from its initial failures.

The Lehman Brothers breakdown reveals how the basic assumptions that underlie rational decision-making theory can lead to the breakdown of learning. Lehman illustrates the prevailing belief that organizations can overcome many disasters, crises, and breakdowns simply by improving the degree to which they make rational decisions. Table 8.1 provides an overview of the different approaches to decision making, including their primary sources of information, the situation in which they work best, and their limitations, and benefits.

RATIONAL DECISION MAKING

Rational decision making describes a process in which individuals or a group of individuals systematically weigh various choices by calculating the probability of success for each choice. Rational decision making relies on two key beliefs about what constitutes the best decisions. First, decision makers must be objective, which means the decision maker eliminates, as much as possible, emotions, perceptual biases, and other psychological biases. Because emotions and bias can lead to less than optimal decisions, decision makers turn to systematic tools like mathematics, statistical models, and other quantitative measures to make the best decisions. The second belief is that decision makers must have access to perfect information—that is, all the necessary and accurate information from the environment that is needed to inform the decision. The less perfect the information and the less objective the decision maker, the more likely the decision will be less than optimal. The more a decision maker deviates from being rational and objective, the less desirable the decision. Simply put, according to the rational perspective, decision making requires weighing options, making measured judgments, and calculating mathematical probabilities before taking action.

The Limits of Rational Decision Making

Actual decision making in organizations cannot live up to the standards of perfect rationality and objectivity described by rational decision making; this argument has been made for decades. For example, in some cases the decision maker is faced with only one realistic option or may work under tight time and resource constraints. Further, a decision may be marked with a variety of unforeseen or

Table 8.1. COMPARING AND CONTRASTING DIFFERENT APPROACHES TO DECISION MAKING

	Decision process	Primary source of information	Situation best applied in	Limitations	Benefits
Rational decision making	Carefully weighing various choices, calculating probabilities, and taking the action with the highest probability of success	Probability that an event will come out as expected	Decisions that are routine or standard, when outcomes can be predicted and easily measured	Requires significant amounts of data to predict accurately, since complex problems require complex statistical models; occurs post hoc; does not account for low-probability, high-impact events	Builds models that include the best data available
Behavioral-economic–based decision making	Responding to external incentives that maximize self-interest	Framing of a problem, certainty of outcome, and perceived incentive	Situations in which incentives lead to specific behaviors	Explains behavior but not underlying motivations	Shows how certain incentives motivate behaviors
Organizational decision making	Combining careful weighing of choices and other considerations like politics, culture, and self-interest	Various sources within the organization	Decisions that require a new course of action or change, when exact outcomes cannot be calculated	Is not as accurate as rational decision making	Describes how non-rational elements affect decisions (closer to description of actual decision-making processes)
Experience-based decision making	Drawing on experience and classifying current situation with prior experiences	The situation, mapping the context with prior experiences	Situations that are time critical, whose cause-and-effect links are uncertain, with multiple competing goals	Doesn't always describe how the best decisions are made, but describes how the most experienced people make decisions	Accurately describes how decisions are made under limited time and resources, accounts for complexity of problems
Evidence based	Rely on systematic research results to guide action	Peer reviewed or methodologically proven research	High consensus situations with well defined task	Context, organizational culture, and translation to practice not considered, lack of consenses on what constitutes evidence	Provides data based information to guide decisions

unpredictable consequences, making certainty hard to come by and risk difficult to estimate. Accurate probabilities may be difficult to compute due to the complex and dynamic nature of the variables involved. These factors limit the ability of the decision maker to choose the single best solution.

This perspective holds no preconceived belief that decision making is rational. Rather, decision making is described as a process of justification for actions that have no rational basis. This process of retrospective justification was not lost on John Dewey. He noted that much of human behavior is an attempt to retrospectively justify habits that have no real logical basis. A more contemporary application of Dewey's logic can be found in the research on sensemaking (e.g., Weick, 1993). Although not a decision-making approach, sensemaking describes the process of how people gather information, make judgments, and then take action. Advocates of sensemaking describe how people are prone to look retrospectively at past events in order to make sense of past experiences. Sensemaking offers an alternative viewpoint to rational decision making because it says that decision makers often take action even when they do not have a rational justification for taking action. The key to sensemaking is to understand that once the decision maker takes an action, he or she then seeks an explanation for the action based on a possible repertoire of responses. The contrast between traditional decision making and sensemaking becomes clear. Sensemaking describes decision making as actions in search of justification. With sensemaking, decision making is characterized by "retrospective sensemaking," or looking backward to justify past action. In contrast, rational decision making involves the deliberate weighing of options.

The sensemaking perspective brings to light one of the key problems of rational decision making: There are too few instances in which organizations actually make rational decisions. Rational decision making is a goal to be reached but fails to adequately describe the kinds of decisions that are actually made in organizations on a regular basis. In theoretical terms, rational decision making is a normative theory, describing what should occur but seldom does occur.

EVIDENCE-BASED DECISION MAKING

Evidence-based management was discussed in chapter 2. In some ways, evidence-based decision making is a natural extension of rational decision making because it implies an objective standard to which all decisions in organizations can be applied. In rational decision making, the standard is probability-based mathematical calculation. In evidence-based management, the standard is academic peer-reviewed journals. Despite some promising support from many well-known academics and some well-deserved attention at high-profile academic conferences and journals, there is reason for those interested in learning from experience to remain skeptical of a strict adherence to evidence-based decision-making protocols.

One reason for skepticism is that the application of evidence-based decision making in organizations may actually be quite limited, as evidence-based learning provides guidance mostly in cases in which the science is clear. What constitutes science is a constantly negotiated process. As Morrell (2008) argued, beyond the various practical, epistemological, or technical problems involved with implementing evidence-based decision making, the real challenge is definitions of what constitutes evidence lacks consensus. In other words, there are no agreed-upon criteria for what constitutes evidence or how to determine the quality of the evidence. Unfortunately, for practicing managers, social science is by nature a low-consensus field (Pfeffer, 1993); thus, the applicability of evidence-based management will likely be met with some limitations. Reay, Berta, and Kazman-Kohn (2009) reviewed research from management and found that evidence-based management itself lacks evidence of its own effectiveness.

A second limitation is that those writing on evidence-based approaches to learning tend to treat evidence-based approaches in other fields as well-established practices. Aspiration fields like science and medicine may enjoy a higher degree of consensus than the study of organizations, but even these fields encounter ambiguity. A reading of evidence-based practice in an aspiration field like medicine reveals that evidence-based practice is something that many talk about but few actually practice (Doerr, 2004). Because evidence-based practice is not fully adopted in other fields, it has been challenging for organizational scholars to identify examples and practices that might be applicable for managers in adopting evidence-based learning. As Doerr (2004) has observed, evidence-based practice in medicine has run into several significant roadblocks. Evidence-based practice is time consuming, requires a constant review of academic literature, and often requires significant translation to be applicable to specific situations. Further, the evidence-based research literature is often incomplete and subject to change.

Although challenges to evidence-based practices are often targeted at other fields, many of these challenges also apply to decision making in organizations. A key roadblock to effective evidence-based practice is that few practices in organizational decision making lend themselves to strict interpretations of evidence. Head (2008) argued that management is more about judgment and debate than scientific analysis (see also Mintzberg, 2004). Management decisions will always carry competing interpretations of what constitutes correct action. Management requires understanding of shifting information and assessment of multiple, often-contradictory sources and interpretations of evidence. On epistemological grounds, Cascio (2007) questioned the very process that results in determining what is legitimate evidence and suggested that what evidence-based decision making proposes is to mask the political process of management under the legitimacy of science.

In summary, evidence-based learning offers a promising new approach that may improve the legitimacy of academic research among practicing managers, transform the content of management learning, and shape the core knowledge of practicing managers. Evidence-based learning may apply when situations call for systematic analysis, but it may not work as well in other situations, such as when managers do not have time to consult the latest research, analyze the facts, and challenge conventional wisdom.

BEHAVIORAL ECONOMICS AS DECISION MAKING

In contrast to the rational decision-making approach, which describes a normative or idealized way of making decisions, the behavioral decision-making approach seeks to describe how people actually make decisions. Behavioral-based decision making shares with rational decision making a belief that objective and perfect decision making is possible, but the behavioral approach is more concerned with how actual decisions deviate from purely rational decisions. Behavioral economics blends contemporary psychology with decision making research to expose the mental tricks that individuals use when faced with difficult choices. Behavioral economics has set out to codify the various ways that actual decision making deviates from rational decision making (Akerloff & Shiller, 2010; Becker & Murphy, 2001; Thaler, 1999).

Another deviation from rational decision making occurs through something called "problem framing." Nobel Prize–winning economist Daniel Kahneman (Kahneman, Slovic, & Tversky, 1982) found that the way a situation is framed, or presented, will impact the choices made by decision makers. Recall that rational decision-making processes put a premium on probability that an event will occur. Problem framing describes a tendency of individuals to frame risk differently depending on the potential for loss or gain. Decision makers are more likely to take great risks when trying to recoup losses. On the other hand, decision makers are likely to take less risk when they consider holding on to winners. This results in a tendency of individuals to sell investments like stocks too soon, but hold on to losing investments too long (Kahneman & Tversky, 1979).

Problem framing shows one of the ways that decision makers deviate from rational behavior: They seem unable to accurately and consistently calculate probabilities because they are preoccupied with how a problem is framed. A consistent finding is that when faced with a choice, individuals tend to choose problems framed as "positive" or "gains" over choices framed as "negative" or "losses."

The behavioral approach to decision making has made strides in understanding how decisions are made in organizations; however, its focus has been on how actual behavior deviates from rational behavior. Still the behavioral approach to decision making discounts or ignores the importance of less formal decision-making processes like emotions and intuition (Berg & Gigerenzer,

2010). Another more important problem plagues behavioral-based decision making. Even if we accept the basic premise, that people respond to incentives, it is extremely difficult to predict, let alone design, large-scale systems that effectively incentivize individuals in organizations to make effective decisions that are ultimately in the best interest of the organization. Several examples throughout this book relate the problems associated with compensation systems by even the most advanced organizations, including Enron and Lehman Brothers. The compensation systems were intermingled with significant accounting losses. Even Lehman followed the advice of the most sophisticated rational models and tied its compensation systems directly to shareholder value. Despite the most effective probability-calculating machines, organizations appear to be amateurs at predicting what behaviors will result from various inventive systems (see Kerr, 1995).

ORGANIZATIONAL DECISION MAKING

Organizational decision making emerged in response to some of the limitations of rational decision making (Cyert & March, 1963; March & Simon, 1958; Simon, 1976). Organizational approaches to decision making argue that even behavioral decision making approaches do not adequately account for the context of decision making. For example, the behavioral decision-making approach suggests that in most cases, decision makers' search for perfect information will leave them unsatisfied. Because the cost, in terms of time, money, and other resources, is so great, perfect information is almost never achieved. Instead, decision makers encounter bounded rationality, the process of relying on limited information and time to make a decision. The bounded rationality principle suggests that the perfect rationality and objectivity sought by rational decision makers is never fully achieved, and decision making is always bounded by certain practical constraints.

Influential theorist James March's (1988) often-cited description of decision making in organizations places decisions as "a collection of choices looking for problems, issues and feelings looking for decision situations in which they might be aired, solutions looking for issues to which they might be the answer, and decision makers looking for work" (p. 295). March described decision making as a process that is not always systematic, but rather looks more like a "garbage can into which various problems and solutions are dumped by participants." Decisions arise in organizations as groups of individual decision makers weigh goals and agendas, past organizational practices, available resources, and current incentives. The notion of decision making as a garbage can implies that decision making in most cases is not like the systemic and rational process described by the rational decision-making models. Rather, decision making is infused with emotions, politics, and other nonrational factors.

AN EXPERIENTIAL APPROACH TO DECISION MAKING

Experience-based decision-making approaches provide a compelling alternative. Naturalistic decision making is one approach (Klein, 1999). Naturalistic decision making seeks to describe how managers, teams, and organizations make decisions in natural settings. Some of the first research on naturalistic decision making sought to understand how fire crew chiefs decided what actions to take during fires. The research revealed that fire chiefs did not follow the rules set out by rational decision making research, but drew on years of experience with fires to assess the situation at hand. Rather than weighing various options, as the rational decision-making process would suggest, the fire chiefs were more likely to identify and follow through on one single course of action.

In naturalistic settings, people do not often weigh a series of choices and decipher the probabilities of success for each. These rational activities take too much time and would not yield useful results. Imagine calculating the probability of successfully rescuing someone trapped in a burning building before deciding whether or not to enter! Naturalistic decision making shows that in real settings, decision makers draw on their experience, assess a situation, and then determine a single best course of action from the available data (Klein, 2008). Decision makers scan their environment for relevant information about the situation. Then they classify the situation based on a prototype, an imagined version of the situation that the decision maker has previously encountered. This is especially true in time-critical and complex environments in which choices cannot be methodically weighed or probabilities calculated. All of this is to say that decision makers rely on intuition—the process of assessing a situation, identifying problems or opportunities, and knowing what action to take—even when they cannot consciously describe what is happening. Intuition often involves an immediate emotional and cognitive reaction to a situation.

Growing evidence from psychology and neuropsychology suggests that experience-based decision making is better than rational decision making in describing how the brain actually works. Psychologist Tim Wilson (2004) argued that decision making requires the use of the adaptive unconscious brain. The unconscious mind has a capacity to process information and compare it to history. In fact, he argued that engaging rational decision-making processes actually limits our ability to make effective decisions. Collateral learning, discussed in chapter 1, provides an important consideration. Because most rational processes focus on only bits and pieces of a decision, the number of variables accounted for in any one decision is minimal. Collateral learning engages the unconscious elements of decision making that lead to success. Further, Nobel Prize–winning neuroscientist Eric Kandel's work on the brain shows how learning is a process of constant recollection and history. Because the mind is constantly updating and changing, it is always in a process of "becoming" (see, for example, Kandel, 2012).

AN EXPERIENCE-BASED MODEL OF DECISION MAKING
IN ORGANIZATIONS

An experience-based approach to decision making focuses on the process of learning, adapting, and managing the various tensions inherent in the decision-making process. Decisions are not viewed as one-time events, but rather as a process of continual adjustment, improvement, and adaptation to changing circumstances. The experiential approach integrates rational and evidence-based learning with experience-based perceptions and naturalistic learning. An experience-based model of learning involves six reoccurring steps.

Step 1: Assess the Context

The first step in an experiential-based process of decision making involves assessing the context. The assessment moves along two dimensions. The first dimension assesses the operational environment—whether it is novel, that is, never faced before, or routine, faced many times. The distinction between routine and novel operating environments was discussed in earlier chapters. The second dimension assesses the task complexity and nature of the problem. Task complexity is determined by taking note of the number of variables, the dynamic nature of the variables, and their potential interactions (Campbell, 1988). The nature of the problem concerns whether the problem is well structured or ill structured.

A well-structured problem involves

- A single goal
- Agreement among observers that the situation is adequately solved or has the potential to be adequately solved

An ill-structured problem involves

- No consensus about what constitutes success
- Difficulty in defining the nature of the problem itself

In human factors approaches to decision making, this step is often referred to as "situational awareness" (Endsley, 1995). Situational awareness focuses on the operational environment and does not capture one's broader outlook or general disposition to one's environment. From the viewpoint of learning, this step implies a distinct epistemology of decision making rather than simply an operational assessment (King & Kitchener, 1994). In most cases, decision makers will quickly realize that they operate in an ill structured, complex, and novel environment, a situation that renders traditional approaches to decision making less useful.

Step 2: Consider Outcomes in Context

In the second step, desired outcomes are stated and considered in context. This step often involves groups of individuals representing different backgrounds, functional areas, or interests. Rather than setting specific, measurable goals, the group outlines a variety of potential outcomes and competing demands. The emphasis is not on seeking consensus, agreement, or shared goals, but on identifying competing demands and competing commitments that are inherent in the decision-making processes. Rather than seeking consensus, tradeoffs are identified. Rather than seeking agreement, disagreements are aired. Rather than seeking shared goals, multiple, often competing goals are put on the table. Step 2 is a difficult process, but seeks to more realistically define the environment that is faced.

Step 3: Identify Potential Unintended Consequences of Action

Step 3 involves identifying various unintended consequences of action. The process is also known as identifying "second- and third-order consequences." The specific unintended consequences are less important to this process because the real goal is to psychologically prime the decision maker to the realistic possibility that the action will not go as planned. This step involves an epistemology as well, as it helps facilitate understanding that decisions are not always rational and that cause-and-effect relations are difficult to gauge with accuracy in these kinds of environments.

Step 4: Assess Worst-Case Scenarios

Step 4 involves identifying worst-case scenarios and identifying "stop rules." Identifying worst-case scenarios helps to further prime decision makers as to the potential adverse consequences of decisions. Stop rules serve as external indicators that the decision is off track and that serious re-evaluation must take place. Stop rules are common in manufacturing, where serious operational problems can impact quality or safety, but stop rules are rarely used in managerial decision making.

Step 5: What Does the Evidence Say?

Step five requires reviewing evidence, including data gathered as part of normal operating procedures. Organizations often enact data collection practices and reviews internal data provides an important aspect of learning. Even more important, evidence from outside the organization, including qualitative data gathered from industry groups, competitors, and government data all provide insights into the potential vulnerabilities. Most organizations have already mastered evidence based learning as part of their data analytics practices and ongoing decision making processes.

Step 6: Update, Revise, Be Resilient, and Respond to Breakdown

Step 6 occurs after the initial decision has been made and involves updating, re-evaluation, and adjustment. It may be the most important but most neglected step in the decision-making process. Updating is important because it takes the linear process of decision making and transforms it into a cycle of learning.

This six-step process provides a method to apply a more complete theory of decision making based on experiential learning. The process addresses several of the weaknesses that have been identified by research on decision making, which include weak cause-and-effect links, unrealized unintended consequences, multiple possible interpretations of information, and multiple competing goals within the organization.

CONCLUSION

This chapter has reviewed and critiqued various approaches to decision making and offered an alternative based on experiential learning. The experiential approach has several advantages over traditional decision-making approaches because it is not based simply on observed behavior, but integrates recent understanding of cognitive and emotional processes and how they relate to decision making. The six-step process of decision making by experience describes a holistic process of learning because it requires the recognition and appreciation of emotions, cognitions, and actions in the decision-making process. Future research and observation will help identify specific processes associated with each step.

SECTION III
Building Resilience through Learning

CHAPTER 9

Case Study: Learning from the Search for Weapons of Mass Destruction in Iraq

PREFACE TO THE BREAKDOWN

How could they have been so wrong?[1] Twelve months ago, all the evidence had pointed in one direction. The firsthand accounts, the satellite imagery, the detailed drawings and mockups—everything had fallen into place. The case was beyond solid, so they thought. The sure-fire prediction was that the Iraqis held the capability to make biological-grade weapons—weapons that Saddam Hussein and his henchmen could put to use with just 45 minutes' notice—but over the course of the last few months, the sure-fire prediction had changed. After weeks of inspecting, visiting nearly 100 sites across Iraq, interviewing more than 60 people, and reviewing thousands of documents, the evidence now pointed in a completely different direction. As the analysts[2] began their journey home from the airport just outside Baghdad, they faced the empty desert. They had followed the data, looked honestly at the situation, even fought against those who disagreed. They had risked their reputations on a set of assumptions, but in the end the assumptions had proved wrong.

Coming to the conclusion that they, and others, had miscalculated the presence of biological weapons in Iraq proved one of the most difficult experiences they would encounter. As loyal employees of the U.S. Central Intelligence Agency (CIA), the analysts proudly served their country, but questions swirled through their head. How had they miscalculated so completely? By the summer of 2004, the analysts would now have to convince the others—superiors, peers, and even the public—that they too had been deceived. Learning, the primary function of a knowledge-based organization like an intelligence agency, had broken down.

A detailed recounting of the events surrounding the search for weapons of mass destruction in Iraq reveal how many in the intelligence community came to learn that the weapons of mass destruction in Iraq were not as they had predicted. By piecing together publically available documents, a new look at the events emerges. The events are described in terms of four stages of organizational breakdown: incubation, precursor events, full-scale breakdown, and rebuilding. The role that resilience played in the aftermath of the events is also explored. The events provide a useful case to study organizational learning and resilience because the organizations represent the various political, bureaucratic, cultural, and historical barriers to learning that confront contemporary organizations.

STAGE 1: INCUBATION

In August 2003, the summer heat at the CIA's headquarters in Langley, Virginia, felt oppressive. A walk of just a few hundred yards from the parking lot to the massive office complex left employees drenched in sweat. As nervous as the Northern Virginia traffic may have already made the analysts that morning, the information they were about to review put them even more on edge. It was a good thing some within the agency shunned coffee; a little caffeine might work their nerves just a bit too much. Several analysts would soon be at the center of a lesson in the breakdown of learning in organizations, a breakdown that would become very public. This would be especially troubling because people in the intelligence community don't enter the spotlight willingly.

In August 2002, Western citizens were learning more and more about the potential for mass casualties inflicted by evil forces around the world. Chemical weapons could choke a person to death almost instantly. A crude nuclear bomb, kludged together with uranium foraged from a common household fire detector and a simple detonator, could cause massive deaths and suffering. Biological weapons like anthrax and botulism could overwhelm a population; thousands could die before a diagnosis was even made. The acronym WMD, which stood for weapons of mass destruction, found its way into casual conversation as surely as did the latest exploits of celebrities.[3]

Just a few days before, the U.S. vice president had described how Saddam Hussein, the black fedora–wearing, shotgun-toting dictator of Iraq, continued to build weapons that could lead to mass casualties directly on U.S. soil. "There is no doubt that Saddam Hussein now has weapons of mass destruction. There is no doubt he is amassing them to use," the vice president told a group of veterans.[4] He made it clear: If the 9/11 attacks on New York and the Pentagon were the worst terrorist attacks to reach U.S. soil, Saddam had the capacity and the intent for much worse.

No one could be more concerned about WMD than the CIA analysts working on WMD. They knew the dangers of WMD as well as any, and they followed the developments in Iraq closely. Many weapons specialists worked at WINPAC, the CIA director's Center for Weapons Intelligence, Nonproliferation, and Arms Control. As the name suggested, WINPAC identified and tracked WMD. Even though the team of analysts sat in the air-conditioned basement of the Langley headquarters, they would soon be in the heat of the breakdown.[5]

Typically, intelligence analysts gather raw information and then subject this information to a number of rigorous analytical reviews, transforming it into an intelligence "product." In some cases, this can take years. Products include papers, pamphlets, or reports. Intelligence officials produce information for intelligence "customers," among whom are policymakers, advisors, and other officials.[6] If deemed acceptable, the intelligence might eventually arrive at the office of George Tenet, director of the CIA. Director Tenet set up WINPAC to report directly to him, effectively bypassing the normally lengthy and bureaucratic process of converting raw data into an intelligence product. With WINPAC, information slid through the bottlenecks of reviewers and analysts and moved quickly to the top. In light of recent threats to U.S. security, the importance of WINPAC had become clear. Even a short delay in getting raw information to a customer might result in disaster, as had happened with 9/11.

Analysts within WINPAC review classified documents on their computers. The sunny August morning that greeted them as they entered the building was now a distant memory. The windowless basement in which they sat encouraged them to focus on the work at hand. Pulling raw data from a number of sources, their task was to build as complete a picture as possible from the morass of information available to them. Despite the potential to become saturated in information, much of what the analysts knew about Iraq's capabilities came from existing intelligence sources. One important source of information was the weapons inspections of UNSCOM—the United Nations Special Commission on Iraq—which was conducting extensive on-the-ground surveys for WMD programs in Iraq. The analysts might be inclined to conclude that UNSCOM consistently found evidence of WMD in Iraq, because over the years UNSCOM had developed a particular mindset on Iraq—a loosely held hypothesis that the country held an active program to create and deploy biological WMD. Analysts within the CIA also took this position. The recent past was in the forefront of their minds. They recalled how surprised they had been after the 1991 invasion of Iraq by U.S.-led forces to learn how much progress Saddam Hussein had made in developing chemical and biological weapons. Close observers knew that Saddam had developed and used chemical weapons several times during his reign. The CIA knew that he had these weapons. In 1991, however, the analysts and others at the CIA were caught off-guard by the degree of sophistication Saddam possessed in developing and delivering WMD. Their surprise was compounded by the realization that, by some estimates, Saddam sat less than a year away from the ability to build a crude nuclear bomb. The progress Saddam had made had shocked everyone. Now, in the post-9/11 era, the WINPAC analysts vowed not be tricked again.

Threats Posed by Biological Weapons

Nuclear capability was one thing, but the group of analysts felt concerned over the low-grade approach to terror, the targeting of a small group of people that would bring terror to hundreds of thousands, possibly even millions of people, without an explosion. On the screens of their secure computer network, the analysts pulled up images of known biological weapons plants. These included pictures the CIA had acquired from surveillance satellites. Sitting at their desks the analysts thought about the science of biological weapons manufacturing. They knew, as any analyst knew, that with just a little work, Saddam's men could grow biological toxins like anthrax or botulism on a grand scale. These could easily be transported and spread as a crude but effective form of WMD.

Key analysts in WINPAC had been studying pieces of Iraq's biological weapons capability for nearly a decade. Now they wanted to build a complete picture. Since the 1991 invasion of Iraq, surveillance data from Iraq was greater than ever before thanks to advanced technology, including satellite imagery. Information also came in through the United Nations–sponsored weapons inspections. Through these inspections, the CIA had access to firsthand observations of various potential WMD sites within Iraq.[7]

What the WINPAC analysts needed, however, was human source intelligence, abbreviated as HUMIT—a somewhat inexact science of getting individuals to give you information. In most cases, human intelligence rests on the direct information given to analysts by individuals who have inside access. The human intelligence gathering programs include many different facets. One type of human intelligence gathering involves interrogating a captured spy, a defector, or a member of a terror group. In many cases human intelligence gathering involves recruiting insiders to collect and pass on information about an organization's activities. This might involve recruiting a disgruntled employee who is willing to pass on insider information.

In the search for WMD, CIA analysts were hungry, if not desperate, for more HUMIT on Iraq's WMD program. One file remained of great interest because it contained human source information that proved particularly valuable to the U.S. intelligence effort. The source came from within the inner circle of Iraq's weapons programs and promised a unique look inside Iraq's "death machines on wheels," portable biological weapons–making machines. What the information from this source offered was no less than an invitation to go to war.

Congressional Briefing by Central Intelligence Agency Deputy Director John McLaughlin on Weapons of Mass Destruction

The U.S. Senate Select Committee on Intelligence is responsible for oversight of the CIA and is the official interface between the intelligence community and the U.S. Senate. At a closed-door meeting of the committee on October 2, 2002, George Tenet, director of the CIA, testified. Next to him sat John McLaughlin, deputy director of the CIA, who had more than 25 years of experience as a CIA analyst. The senators grilled the two men, Tenet, a lifelong Washington insider and former congressional aide, and McLaughlin, among the most respected analysts in the CIA. The senators wanted to know what Tenet and McLaughlin knew about Iraqi WMD. Senator Levin asked, "If [Saddam] did not feel threatened, is it likely that he would initiate an attack using a weapon of mass destruction?"

> "My judgment would be that the probability of him initiating an attack—let me put a time frame on it—in the foreseeable future, given the conditions we understand now, the likelihood I think would be low," McLaughlin responded.
>
> "Now if he did initiate an attack you've indicated," Senator Levin pressed on, "he would probably attempt clandestine attacks against us.... But what about his use of weapons of mass destruction? If we initiate an attack and he thought he was in extremis or otherwise, what's the likelihood in response to our attack that he would use chemical or biological weapons?"
>
> "Pretty high, in my view," McLaughlin responded.[8]

Professor Jerrold Post had been saying the same thing publicly for some time.[9] A psychiatrist by training, Post created and had directed the Center for the Analysis of Personality and Political Behavior at the CIA for more than 20 years. Now a professor at George Washington University, he had developed a reputation among both universities and the intelligence community for his approach to psychological assessment. Dr. Post and a small group of peers had virtually invented a systematic approach to assessing national threats by looking into the minds and behaviors of world leaders. Post had studied Saddam Hussein for decades and compared his findings on Saddam with what he knew about other world leaders. Hussein may be ruthless, Post concluded, but he is not a madman. Saddam would not put himself in a position to knowingly put his rule at risk, but if Hussein believed his position as a world leader was threatened, he would stop at nothing to keep himself in power.

McLaughlin's comments simply confirmed Post's diagnosis of Hussein. Saddam wasn't unpredictable; he could not have stayed in power for more than 34 years if he wasn't a judicious political calculator. But it was one thing for a retired CIA psychiatrist to make such a judgment and another thing for the standing deputy director of the CIA to make that claim. McLaughlin echoed Post's assessment. Saddam Hussein would not go down in the last flaming bunker if he had a way out, but he could be extremely dangerous and would stop at nothing if he was backed into a corner. If he believed his very survival as a world-class political actor was threatened, Saddam could respond with unrestrained aggression, using whatever weapons and resources were at his disposal, in what would surely be a "tragic and bloody" final act.[10]

Learning as a Shell Game

Hanging on the wall of CIA Deputy Director John McLaughlin's office was, reports say, a reproduction of Hieronymus Bosch's painting "The Conjurer." The picture depicts the shell game, the ultimate trick of deception. More commonly known as the ball and cup trick, in this game the magician lays out three cups in front of a willing observer. The magician lifts each cup to show the observer that there is nothing hidden underneath. Then he places a tiny ball under one of the cups. He proceeds to shift, slide, swipe, slip, and shimmy the three cups around the table. He then asks the unwitting observer to decipher which cup conceals the ball. This is difficult because the cups have all moved positions several times, and each cup looks the same. Most of the time the observer believes he can correctly track the ball as it travels through the magician's slight of hand. Such confidence is not warranted. The observer makes his judgment. Without hesitation, the magician lifts the ball to reveal an empty cup. The trick is based on deception, as the magician has clandestinely removed the ball from under the cup.

Few people knew better than McLaughlin, an accomplished magician, the games that dictators play. Saddam played the shell game with weapons inspectors year in, year out. Saddam consistently and effectively foiled inspector efforts to prove Iraq was building WMD. Saddam's vacillations—often forcing the inspectors to leave the country at a moment's notice, appearing to cooperate, then failing to cooperate with them at other times—only increased suspicions. The inspectors and the analysts who supported them faced a shell game. But what kind of shell game was Saddam playing? Inspectors continued to come up empty in their searches, but the failure to find WMD only left them feeling uneasy. How could they ever know if biological WMD existed in Iraq?

The inspectors were further perplexed by history. In 1995, weapons inspectors discovered that Saddam had rebuilt his chemical and biological weapons program. From a scientific standpoint, chemical and biological weapons were easy to build and put into weapons. The problem was delivery. Short of a suicide mission by a pilot who would inevitably become contaminated as he sprayed weapons from his plane, there were few ways to reliably deliver such a destructive payload. Saddam shunned missiles because poisons and biological matter needed to be sprayed.

To achieve this, the analysts had surmised that Saddam's scientists decided to design and build an unmanned aircraft that would fly using a remote navigational mapping system. The plane would be equipped with two large tanks fitted with sprayers to deliver the poison. The sprayers too would be controlled remotely. The system was even equipped with the latest up-to-date global positioning software.[11]

Evidence began to accumulate. Physical evidence such as Saddam's unmanned drones suggested WMD, but without inside sources analysts could not get their hands on the specific type of information they needed. What they needed to make a strong case was an inside source. The CIA found this source in an Iraqi defector. The defector's stories of mobile death machines provided verifiable data on the existence of WMD in Iraq. The man was not, however, a CIA "asset," the term used for a person who was a source of valuable information. The asset belonged to the German Federal Intelligence Service, known as the BND, which is short for the Bundesnachrichtendienst. The only contact the CIA had with this asset was through an analyst who worked at the Defense Intelligence Agency (DIA), the intelligence arm of the U.S. Department of Defense. In other words, the CIA had no direct link to this asset; they only knew about him through documents and reporting handed to them, and even these were secondary sources.

Not only did the CIA not have direct access to the asset, it also lacked a sense of trust with the Germans. The relationship between the German and the U.S. intelligence communities remained one of distrust, despite growing cooperation in recent years. During the Cold War, the CIA feared that the Stasi, the East German intelligence service, had infiltrated the BND. Decades after the end of the Cold War, the CIA remained skeptical of information provided by the BND. And even as the two communities began to share information, like two companies after an uncomfortable merger, both remained suspicious of the other. Skepticism played a natural role in the game these organizations played.

Initially, CIA requests to interview the asset directly were denied by the BND. It was not common practice for one intelligence service to let another interview its assets, but the BND claimed another reason for not allowing an interview: Their asset hated Americans. He would never agree, according to his BND handlers, to speak directly with a U.S. government official. So there was a degree of shock when the BND changed its mind and allowed U.S. intelligence officers an opportunity to meet the valuable former Iraqi in May 2000. But this was nothing compared with the shock they received when they interviewed the asset firsthand. The name of the asset: Curveball.[12]

STAGE 2: PRECURSOR EVENTS

The Source Called "Curveball"

The dark-haired, mustached Iraqi entered Munich, Germany, with a tourist visa in November 1999. Pleading with German authorities not to send him back to

Iraq, he was granted political asylum. He claimed he was in great danger if he was sent back and that powerful people were after him. The Germans had heard many stories like this; there was nothing unique about this man. The German authorities then shipped him off to a former Soviet refugee camp in the Bavarian town of Zirndorf.

Life in the refugee camp may not have been what the boisterous but charming Iraqi had envisioned. His story quickly grew more interesting. The man owed money to powerful people and had access to them because of his position within the Iraqi elite. He told how he had come to be included in some secret dealings. With the growing revelation of this man's importance, German intelligence officers grew eager to hear his story. They became particularly fascinated with his talk of WMD.

The Iraqi explained how he had graduated at the top of his class at the university in Iraq. He explained how he had demonstrated strong academic promise. The man had studied chemistry, a highly sought-after specialty. Before his graduation, the Ba'ath party, Saddam Hussein's power base from which he controlled Iraq, had recruited him. He began to work on one of the country's most elite, secret, and promising weapons programs. Soon he was designing and overseeing the construction of a highly secretive project.

The Iraqi refugee proved to be an important find for the BND. With apparent access to some of the deepest secrets of the Iraqi weapons programs, he quickly became one of the BND's prime sources of human-source intelligence. Over the next several months, BND agents met with the Iraqi on countless occasions and gathered some of the most important, detailed, and nerve-shredding information that had yet to be obtained about Iraq's weapons programs. He told of Iraq's deepest military secrets and of Iraq's desire to manufacture WMD.

During the many long hours of questioning with German officials, the stories remained consistent. Because the Iraqi defector did not speak English and his German was poor, BND officials debriefed him in his native Arabic tongue. Many individuals came and went during the briefings. The fact that the Iraqi spoke only in Arabic was inevitably frustrating to his handler. Usually, a handler preferred to debrief his asset directly, without the awkwardness and unreliability of a translator. Too much information became lost in translation. Besides, the relationship between a handler and his asset can be an intimate one, one of dependence, power, and odd loyalties—although in this case it was not always clear who held the power at which precise moment, the handler or the asset.

In the debriefing interviews, the Iraqi showed his charming side. He actively engaged with the BND officials who debriefed him. He appeared to enjoy his conversations. He loved to engage his audience. The Germans became increasingly pleased with their source. He talked. They liked what they heard. They wanted to hear more, and they offered the Iraqi what he wanted in return, as they moved him from the crowded refugee housing to a more comfortable place. The informant remained confident and sure of his ability to provide useful information. This confidence spilled over to his BND handlers. The BND officials were mesmerized. Over the course of nearly 100 interviews, the Iraqi's story held up, and he became a key source of human intelligence. What the man offered proved helpful not only to the Germans, but also to intelligence services around the world. The Iraqi quickly became a prized asset.

A source like this one could make an intelligence officer's career. At a minimum, it is likely that the main handler within the German secret service rose from an insignificant position in the BND to one with a much higher profile. With such incentives, the German intelligence officers in charge of cultivating the asset built faith in him. As one U.S. official later explained, "The [handler] had fallen in love with his asset and the asset could do no wrong. I mean [according to the BND case officer], the story [told by the asset] was 100% correct."[13]

By early 2000, news of the dark-haired Iraqi defector reached the DIA office in Berlin, probably through the British intelligence service known as MI6. The DIA served as the principal U.S. military intelligence-gathering office in Europe. Over the years, U.S. intelligence officials have used the suffix "ball" to identify human intelligence sources related to weapons. The DIA gave the Iraqi the nickname "Curveball," a term from American baseball. It describes the way the ball flies through the air as it moves from the pitcher's hand and crosses in front of the batter. When the pitcher throws a curveball, he intentionally tries to deceive the batter and entice him to swing at the pitch, which unexpectedly curves out of place just before crossing the plate. The batter swings and, if the plan works, ends up swinging at air as the ball curves out of range of the batter's swing.

The BND reports provided detailed accounts of Iraqi biological weapons programs but only basic information on the source Curveball. The DIA officer who received the information pressed his BND contact for more. What was his background? Where did he study? With whom did he work? Was he related to anyone important? When could I meet with him?

News of Curveball made its way to the desks of analysts at WINPAC. The text was difficult to make out at times, because the briefings had been translated and re-translated. Yet, in the end, Curveball's story confirmed a widely held belief: In a nutshell, Iraq had WMD.

The Meeting with Curveball

Despite the growing belief within the CIA that Curveball provided valuable information, some analysts remained skeptical about his credibility. He might well be providing good information, but could his story really be trusted if he later proved to be a con man? CIA analysts made it their job to be skeptical, and nowhere was there more skepticism than with human intelligence.[14]

Without firsthand contact with the asset, analysts could only guess at the truth of the story they had heard. This skepticism led the WINPAC team to request a direct meeting with Curveball. The request, made through the DIA contact who was handling the information on Curveball, landed dead. The DIA analyst would not even entertain the request. "Who do the CIA think they are to ask to see our source?" he was overheard saying.

When the BND finally allowed the DIA to interview Curveball, Curveball was nursing a hangover.[15] His physical and mental state surprised the unnamed intelligence analyst when he finally got the chance to meet Curveball face to face. In order to hide his identity from the asset, the analyst posed as a German official so as not to arouse Curveball's suspicions. If the guy truly hated Americans, a meeting with a U.S. intelligence official might end the whole relationship between Curveball and the Germans in an instant. Thus, the agent, a German-looking American, became the first U.S. official to meet Curveball face to face.

One of the key pieces of information that would solidify Curveball's credibility lay in his testimony about the biological weapons accident that killed many people. German officials had agreed to let the agent draw a sample of Curveball's blood. If Curveball had indeed been infected by the anthrax accident as he claimed, he would have built up antibodies that fight off the bacterial infection caused by the anthrax poisoning. It was also possible that as a key engineer working on the project, Curveball could have been vaccinated against the harmful effects of anthrax. Whether he had been exposed to or vaccinated against the bacteria, his body would show the permanent mark of infection. In other words, if Curveball was telling the truth and had been exposed to anthrax, his body would have built a natural marker to prove it. The test came up negative—but the problem with the anthrax testing administered by the analyst was that it provided a lot of false-negatives. In other words, it was possible that Curveball had been exposed to anthrax, but the opposite was also possible.

The analyst experienced another surprise: Curveball spoke English. It was broken English, to be sure, less than perfect, but English nevertheless. This discovery came as a surprise because all the information the analyst had received to this point suggested a man who spoke mostly Arabic and struggled with German. The Germans had told the analyst that Curveball hated Americans and would not speak to them. The Germans had said that Curveball did not speak any English. But here was Curveball now speaking English.

The Reluctant German

Even after years running overseas posts for the CIA, the race for WMD seemed to have stressed CIA Agent Tyler Drumheller in an unusual way. He was meeting his contact at a Georgetown restaurant, the Sea Catch, which is located on a small side street just off of M Street. It was the choice location for his contact, "Gradl,"[16] who was now the head of a German intelligence unit stationed in the United States. Gradl claimed to have sat in the back of the room and observed as

Curveball charmed his handlers. Having been in direct contact with Curveball, Gradl appeared reluctant to endorse Curveball's credibility as a legitimate source of human intelligence. According to government documents, as well as Drumheller's personal account, the German officer claimed he would deny it if it ever came out, but German intelligence had a lot of doubts about this guy Curveball. He was a very erratic character, and they had to move him a couple of times. Gradl argued that Curveball represented only a single source whose reporting could not be validated. Personally, Gradl claimed he thought Curveball could be a fabricator. It's not really worth the time to meet him, Gradl argued.

The Determination of the Credibility of Curveball

When Drumheller relayed this information to the analysts working on the intelligence side of the CIA, a firestorm ensued.[17] A flurry of heated meetings exploded across Langley. Finally, after weeks of meetings without any progress, Drumheller's assistant called a meeting on December 19. Government documents[18] cited a meeting in which CIA officials came to an official decision to endorse the intelligence offered by Curveball. The meeting included at least four CIA officials: Drumheller's assistant for the regional chief for operations in Europe; an analyst from the CIA's WINPAC group on the intelligence side; an assistant for John McLaughlin, deputy director of the CIA; and a member of the clandestine operations group who specialized in WMD.

The WINPAC analyst offered the assessment that Curveball had access to important information. The operations member countered with his doubts that Curveball had been more forthcoming and cooperative when he needed resettlement assistance. Now that he did not need it, Curveball was less helpful, possibly because when he was being helpful, he was embellishing a bit. The German BND had developed doubts about him, the operations chief explained, recounting Drumheller's discussion with Gradl. Also, CIA operations had not been able to vet him operationally and still knew very little about him. The intelligence community had corroborated portions of his reporting with open source information. It seems Curveball may have provided information that he had downloaded from the Internet. With this information in mind, the operations side concluded that Curveball's story could not be trusted.

The WINPAC analyst challenged this assertion. WINPAC analysts had been able to confirm Curveball's story and had evidence to back it up. The Iraqi provided graphic detail. What he described was deemed technically accurate: The weapons could all be manufactured and delivered just as he claimed. In addition, the WINPAC analyst confirmed that others could corroborate his story. Curveball's information provided the strongest human source intelligence they had. The analyst likely realized that the case for WMD in Iraq must not get lost in a bureaucratic turf war. The consequences were much too high. The analysts had been wrong before about Iraqi WMD. They had underestimated Iraq's capabilities in 1995 and sought not to make the same mistake again. Curveball was the best they had. As it turned out, he was about all they had.

The operations analyst could not let this go. The CIA operations people knew that they would be held responsible for the failure to properly assess Curveball's credibility. Even with this in the calculation, Curveball's information had to be factored into their assessment of the case. Sure, Curveball seemed to be a valuable source, yet no one in the operations group was going to vouch for Curveball. Besides, operations did not even own Curveball. Curveball was a Department of Defense source. Okay, as an analyst, you are the master of the case, they seemed to say in the meeting. Ultimately it's your judgment, the operations representative conceded. The problem had been resolved. McLaughlin's assistant believed that the analysts had made the stronger case. Drumheller next took his skepticism of Curveball to his boss, Jim Pavitt, who was heading up the operations directorate at the time. In the end, Curveball was deemed a credible source of human intelligence, despite the dissenting views.

STAGE 3: BREAKDOWN

Compiling the Evidence into the National Intelligence Estimate

One notable intelligence product, and one central to the WMD case, came in the form of the *National Intelligence Estimate: Iraq's Continuing Programs for Weapons of Mass Destruction*—in short, the October NIE. Generally speaking, an NIE document gathers and processes information from across different directors, different desks, and different agencies in an attempt to identify a comprehensive picture of a region, country, or situation. National Intelligence Estimates often mark the first time specific pieces of intelligence are compiled in one document. In most cases, only a few very high-ranking intelligence officers have access to details across the various intelligence organizations. An NIE, however, is a consensus document that requires individuals, who in many cases have never communicated on the subject before, to compile a comprehensive, detailed study. In the case of the Iraq NIE, the document marked the first time all the intelligence about Iraq had been gathered in one place.

One of the senior officials tasked with compiling the intelligence that went into the NIE in Iraq, the first comprehensive account of Iraq's WMD efforts, was a 28-year CIA veteran named Dr. Paul Pillar. With a doctorate from Princeton and a natural tendency for systematic thinking, he had become a highly respected analyst at the agency. As head analyst for the Near East and South Asia, Pillar shared in efforts to compile the intelligence that was included in the final October NIE.[19]

The Role of Power and Politics in Knowledge Interpretation

Pillar felt as if he were in a vise. "We knew we were going to war, we knew that this would be used to make a case for war. But it was our job to produce the Estimate."[20] One senior official even said, "It is the analyst's duty to respond to such requests." Another analyst said that providing information, without hesitation, served as a kind of unspoken oath taken by analysts. Whatever specific information Pillar provided, he knew it would be used to justify the war. The race for WMD had started. There was no turning back.

Pillar felt a second vise closing on him too. He felt pressure coming from both the executive branch (that is, the president and vice president) and the legislative branch (Congress). Both sides continued to reduce "policy questions to intelligence facts." Intelligence informs policy, but intelligence seldom serves as the sole justification for policy. In other words, intelligence usually serves as only a piece of the entire puzzle in developing policy. This was not the case in the race for Iraq's WMD.

Even if the intelligence was not clear, as most intelligence is not, existing information could be construed to look like anything an end user wanted it to look like. Even tiny bits of intelligence can turn into bigger pieces. Having worked on a number of NIEs in the past, as well as countless other intelligence reports, Pillar knew how the process worked. Statements contained in the developing NIE could be easily turned from "judgments" into "facts" if end users had the mind to do so. He had already seen sections of intelligence starting to show up in speeches, television newscasts, and political commentary.

Deep down, most analysts knew that any action to change the situation would have little or no likelihood of stopping the race. Pillar, for example, had written a book on terrorism that made it onto the *Washington Post's* best-seller list. During his years of service as chief analyst for Near East and South Asia, he had built a good reputation within the intelligence community. Outside this close group of colleagues, however, who would care if another CIA analyst quit his job in protest? He would later recall of his decision, "I don't have regrets because I couldn't have gotten out of this, other than resign in protest, but what good would that have done. It wouldn't have mattered if any one of us resigned, the plan was already in place. If I have any regrets, it is allowing intelligence to be used for marketing purposes."

Pillar might have come right out of the CIA history books. In its early days, the agency recruited heavily from Ivy League schools such as Princeton.[21] Unlike today's recruits who may be more likely to see a stint at the agency as a resume builder or launching point to a career in the private sector, Pillar dedicated his entire career to intelligence work. He worked hard as the agency struggled to transform itself from a Cold War bureaucracy into a responsive contemporary organization. Dedicated, long-term employees like Pillar proved one of the mainstays of this successful transition.

As the Cold War came to an end, Pillar found himself at the center of an organization seeking new direction. During the 1980s, most of the action at the CIA occurred within the Russian section. After the breakup of the Soviet Union, Pillar found himself the senior manager running the analytical side of the counterterrorism unit within the CIA. The management system within the unit had emerged during the 1990s in response to the growing concern over terrorism, with most or all the analysts "on loan" from other departments within the CIA. Even though everyone knew of its importance, few saw counterterrorism as a career track. The internal structure made it difficult to gain long-term commitment from many analysts. They saw their careers taking hold in other units. Analysts turned over quickly. After serving a tour in the counterterrorism center, an ambitious analyst would return to a more permanent post within the agency. For Pillar, the personnel system needed improvement.

Pillar built a small coalition within the agency comprised of other units that had the same management problems as his unit. They presented the case to senior management and won. They began to build a permanent analytical group within the counterterrorism center. This proved an important development. Pillar's management coup would provide a model for the CIA as it faced new management challenges and changing threats in the future.

One of the pressures of the post–Cold War era came in the form of time constraints. The pressures to compile the NIE continued to be of consequence to Pillar and the entire team working on it. In most cases, compiling such a document takes months, perhaps years, but the October 2002 NIE on Iraq took less than three weeks. Even so, when Pillar and his peers presented the paper to the U.S. Senate Select Committee on Intelligence, one of the staff members allegedly screamed, "What took you so long!" Despite the pressures involved, Pillar believed his team did the best job they could. He did concede, however, that "the pressure to get it out in such a short time-frame creates certain issues—we had less time to raise doubts and pursue alternatives. We also took a shortcut in there was no outside review. This is a useful and expected step that was left out." In other words, in the normal course of events, a document with the importance of an NIE would be reviewed many times, by many different people—a process that would improve accuracy and contribute to the overall quality of a document.

Pillar was not the only analyst who foresaw problems.[22] Few policymakers had requested official documentation on the connections between Iraq and terrorism beyond the normal annual and semiannual reports mandated by law. Nor had they requested an official document on Iraq WMD. In fact, some felt that many policymakers had specifically avoided requesting an official document on Iraq from the CIA. Even White House policymakers seemed reluctant to ask for an estimate on Iraq. Congress, meanwhile, under the direction of the Select Committee on Intelligence, had pushed forward for the delivery of an NIE on Iraq's WMD. For the development of such a document, the intelligence community's collective efforts would be pulled together on the subject, aided by a database of information, a wealth of experienced analysts and operatives from the region, and an enormous staff dedicated specifically to observing WMD, both in Iraq and around the world.

Instead of utilizing the resources at the CIA, many policymakers at the White House went to other sources for information, relying more heavily on the "intelligence services" offered by Washington area think tanks, such as the American Enterprise Institute or the Pentagon's newly formed Office of Special Plans under Doug Feith. When they did turn to Langley for information, White House policymakers chose informal one-on-one meetings directly with analysts, rather than official assessments such as an NIE. Several times, Vice President Dick Cheney conducted these informal meetings himself, directly probing analysts and putting them on the spot to provide more details on Iraq's WMD programs and connections between Iraq and terrorism.[23]

Another issue to emerge was the process by which intelligence was vetted for use in public speeches. Sometimes, an analyst might not authorize a specific line or quote in a speech—because the source had failed verification, because the source had been discredited, or because new bits of information had changed the way the original information had been interpreted—only to find the lines reinserted in a later draft. Or after cutting lines from one speech, an analyst would later be asked to review another speech containing the same or similar lines. Those within the CIA felt particular pressure on the question of links between terrorism and Iraq when they vetted speeches for officials. They were continually pressed to find information that confirmed a link. Simply leaving questionable information out of a report or making specific notes that communicated a lack of verification proved an exercise in futility. If a document failed to contain enough tidbits of useful intelligence, the document would be returned with a call to "look again," "try harder," "see what else you can dig up."

In other instances, there would be a downright attempt to "spin" a particular line: information phrased to look a certain way, an implication presented but without being clearly stated. Under these circumstances, many analysts found it difficult to provide sound judgment. Time constraints, continual requests for revised assessments, and subtle but clear pressure created a vise—and the pressure would not be letting up soon.

The Destructive Pursuit of an Idealized Goal

The man entered a Pentagon briefing room. The man appeared well educated. He wore a dark suit, dressing the part of his lawyer training. He brought with him a PowerPoint presentation, the briefing format of choice in the Pentagon because the slides presented allowed for quick and succinct summary of ideas, provided visual presentation of ideas, and were easy to use. The technology served as the perfect tool for the Department of Defense headed by a secretary who recommended that all briefings to him last no longer than 15 minutes. It was July 25, 2002.[24]

Douglas Feith directed the Office of Special Plans. The purpose of the office remains unclear. Despite the lack of clarity, Feith's presentation made his agenda quite clear. The title slide read "Assessing the Relationship Between Iraq and al Qaeda."[25] The presentation went on to make a case for a relationship between Iraq and the terrorist group responsible for the 9/11 attacks. It concluded that Iraq and al Qaeda had had numerous contacts over the last decade and that the two groups had collaborated extensively on WMD.

His evidence was thin. His justification for the presentation rested on the notion that the intelligence communities had not taken seriously the connection between Iraq and al Qaeda. He argued that the intelligence community continued to underestimate the threat posed by Iraq and failed to recognize an important link between Saddam Hussein and the terrorist network. Now, with the coerced testimony of Ibn al-Shaykh al-Libi, an al Qaeda terrorist network leader, he had more proof of this deadly relationship.

Intelligence analysts work with raw information often gathered by others. They scrutinize the data, putting it through tests to set context, match sources, and compare the information to what is currently known. By this method they make sense of events. They rely less on conjecture. They consider possibilities and note conflicts in information. They tend to err on the side of caution over extravagance. By nature, analysts are skeptical about information. Through training, they learn not to make claims that cannot be justified. Claims need to be supported by data.

The nature and training of analysts result in judgments that may underestimate threats. A good example of such an underestimate came after the 1991 invasion of Iraq after that country's invasion of neighboring Kuwait. A group of countries led by the United States, and with the blessing of the United Nations, drove the invading Iraqi army back as far as the Iraqi capital of Baghdad. Central Intelligence Agency analysts, crossing the country in the wake of the rout, were shocked to find that Iraq had developed quite an impressive array of WMD. The CIA found chemical, biological, and nuclear weapons programs. They estimated that, without intervention by the United States, Iraq would soon have built an atomic bomb.

However, the CIA struggled to confirm information on Iraq's WMD programs after the coalition troops pulled out. Some became impatient with the wait. None became more frustrated than a select group within the Department of Defense. Although the Defense Department maintains its own intelligence gathering and processing arm—the DIA—both the agency's funding and status remain second to the CIA. The founding fathers of U.S. intelligence specifically designed the DIA to be second also to the CIA when it came to peacetime intelligence. Although British intelligence-gathering efforts actually began in the military—the "MI" in the legendary MI5 and MI6 organizations standing for military intelligence—the founders of the CIA saw a strong intelligence force within the military as a potential conflict of interest. Fearing that a military intelligence service might grow to see the world strictly through military eyes, the creators of the U.S. intelligence service set up the CIA as separate and independent.

The presentation made by Feith served as an official signal that the Department of Defense was seeking to make a case for war independent of the CIA and other intelligence agencies. A Senate-led investigation would later conclude:

> In the case of Iraq's relationship with al Qaeda, intelligence was exaggerated to support Administration policy aims primarily by the Feith policy office, which was determined to find a strong connection between Iraq and al Qaeda, rather than by the IC [intelligence community], which was consistently dubious of such a connection. In order to present a public case that heightened the sense of threat from Iraq, Administration officials reflected more closely the analysis of Under Secretary Feith's policy office rather than the more cautious analysis of the IC.[26]

Preparing the Information

Over the next few months, heated encounters grew throughout the CIA. On the surface, these contentious meetings seemed no different than thousands of heated debates that go on each day in offices around the world—meetings designed to assess the state of projects, put opinions on the table, execute strategy, or carry out objectives. In one in perhaps a thousand unremarkable meetings, some experience emerges that can have a profound effect. A soon-to-occur 72-hour meeting that shuffled between the top floors and the basement of Langley would be a meeting of weight.

Public opinion polls continued to show that Secretary of State Colin Powell remained one of the most respected members of President Bush's cabinet. In fact, Powell ranked as one of the most respected people in the United States. Years of honorable service in the Army had won Powell many supporters and few detractors. He proved a perfect person to lead the charges against Iraq in the United Nations. He turned to Larry Wilkerson as his point man. Even though he had achieved the rank of colonel, Wilkerson displayed the enthusiasm of a first lieutenant. He was easily excited. The cadence of his speech was fast, slowed only by the South Carolina drawl that exposed his southern roots. He emphasized certain words at the expense of others. It tended to show in his eyes, which became wider and more dominant as he hit on key words. As a loyal and trusted friend, he had long served as an advisor to General Colin Powell. After leaving the military, Wilkerson followed Powell to his new role as Secretary of State. Where once they had stood together as soldiers, they now stood as diplomats.

In addition to acting as Powell's chief of staff, Wilkerson led Powell's research team on the question of WMD in Iraq. Central Inteligence Agency Chief George Tenet and John McLaughlin also attended the 72-hour meeting. Most of the meeting allegedly took place in Tenet's spacious conference room on the seventh floor of Langley. Much of the intelligence could only be viewed on special equipment that was located deep in the basement of the building, so Wilkerson found himself shuffling between the two locations for much of the time.

Wilkerson said of the meeting that he "spent five of the most intimate days of my life, and five nights, without sleeping, as did my team, staring into ... the face" of Tenet and McLaughlin. He would also count them as "some of the worst 72 hours of my career."[27] Those involved in the meeting, whether by loyalty, self-deception, or sheer lack of awareness of an alternative, seem to have had already committed to a course of action. As Tyler Drumheller would later remark, "The war was coming.... The administration was looking for intelligence to fit into the policy, to justify the policy."[28]

The meeting was remarkable not just because of its length—nearly 72 hours—but also for those in attendance. Some of the most powerful people in the intelligence and diplomatic community filtered in and out. All the key players were involved. The observations of the CIA analysts and their DIA counterpart who had managed the Curveball case were heard. Information from Gradl, the BND intelligence case officer observing Curveball, was considered, together with the opinions offered by British weapons inspector David Kelly. Central Intelligence Agency Operations Chief Tyler Drumheller's concerns about the credibility of the German intelligence were examined, along with the torture-induced testimony of 9/11 terrorist al-Libi. The details compiled by the Department of Defense's Office of Special Plans under Doug Feith were given time, along with other apparently good intelligence. Throughout the meeting, assorted spies paraded through the conference room at Langley. Weapons inspectors, analysts, operations case managers, and intelligence representatives from other government departments such as the DIA and State Department all made appearances. Intelligence seen by CIA weapons staff strongly supported the argument for Iraq having an active biological weapons program.

At the end of the day stacks of papers and documents lay scattered across the conference room. Among the stacks of paper accumulated at the meeting, sat all the information on Saddam Hussein's weapons programs. During the meeting Wilkerson saw firsthand the explosive pieces of intelligence on Iraq. One piece of information came directly from the interrogation of al-Libi, who pointed to a clear link between Iraq and the al Qaeda terrorist network. A second piece of information came from a military contractor working directly with Iraq. Iraq had acquired the capability to fly an unmanned aircraft capable of spreading biological or chemical weapons. In the course of working with various contractors, Iraq was now in the possession of global positioning system mapping software that included the East Coast of the United States. It appeared that Saddam sought to launch an unmanned aerial attack on this area.

Wilkerson reviewed a number of satellite images with the intensity of a professor. They were photographs of chemical weapons ammunition supply points. The images were consistent with what he already knew. He concluded that the large rusty brown trailers in the images contained chemical weapons and that he was looking at a chemical weapons site. He then reviewed the same satellite photographs taken a few days later. These updated images had two obvious differences: The large rusty trailers allegedly containing chemical weapons were gone and there were now large white vehicles with the black letters "UN," for United Nations, on the top. The UN weapons inspection teams had entered the alleged chemical site. Saddam's men had evidently moved the trailers just in time to evade the UN inspection teams.[29]

Assessing Curveball

The entire Curveball file was also on hand. The presentation included the schemas, graphics, and pictures drawn up from the testimony of Curveball. Despite some feelings within the intelligence community that Curveball was unreliable, presenters stated their belief that his testimony could be trusted. They proceeded to present four reasons why Curveball provided valuable and verified information.

His Trustworthiness

He had described his academic achievements and how he was recruited to oversee the design and construction of biological weapons facilities throughout Iraq. His story had been endorsed by several intelligence services across the globe.

His Expertise

He had proved to be an expert in biological weapons. His elaborate and detailed descriptions of biological weapons had provided a deep and disturbing insight into the scientific knowledge and advanced capacity of Iraq's WMD program. He had described mobile weapons trailers capable of manufacturing large amounts of biological weapons. These trailers looked like standard production vehicles for farm fertilizers or other commonly used industrial chemicals, but they could be converted into mobile death machines within 45 minutes; and they could incubate materials such as smallpox, anthrax, and other biological weapons.

His Detailed Information

Further boosting both his credibility and his expertise, he had provided precise locations of these death machines on wheels and emphatically argued that 12 of these sites were already in production. More importantly, he had described the Djerf al-Naddaf facility, where the mobile factory could enter one side of a building as farm equipment and exit the other end as a death machine. This comic-book image of a vehicle entering into one end of a machine and out through another became known as "traversing."

His Experience

The man had described an industrial accident in which the testing of one mobile anthrax facility exploded, killing 12 scientists. Although present during the accident, he had escaped unharmed. He, like some other scientists, had been vaccinated against the disease.[30]

In the end, a short pile of "good intelligence" rested on a conference table in the middle of the room. All the other information, which failed to uphold the case, remained scattered throughout the conference room. Despite the strong evidence, Wilkerson remained skeptical, if for no other reason than the time pressure the team had been under to get the speech to the UN together. He later recalled: "I felt I wished I could have more time. How could we be asked to justify what would amount to the Normandy invasion in 5 days of preparation?" But when Wilkerson and Powell requested more time, they ran across an uncooperative group of advisors to the president. Wilkerson noted that one advisor said, "We couldn't extend the date because we announced it publicly already."[31] In other words, she implied it would look bad to back down because the race had already begun.

The 72-hour vetting session eliminated many pieces of intelligence that were deemed as unreliable. For example, information that alleged a meeting between an Iraqi intelligence officer and Mohammad Atta, leader in the 9/11 attacks on the United States, was deemed unreliable, and Powell stripped the reference from his speech. Near the end, their vetting of the mountains of intelligence data left only a short stack of papers. This small stack of credible items signified a horrific story of Iraq's past deeds and future intentions.[32] In the end, the meeting would be one of consequence, not just for all those involved, but for the country as well.

The Presentation to the United Nations

The days and nights dragged on, and the case for WMD in Iraq began to solidify. In addition to three days at Langley, the team led by Tenet, McLaughlin,

Wilkerson, and Powell spent nearly two additional days in New York working on the presentation to the United Nations. They operated from a suite in the Waldorf-Astoria Hotel, just a few blocks from UN headquarters in downtown New York City. At the Waldorf, the team continued to review intelligence up until the evening of the UN speech. After the grueling review of the intelligence, one final decision needed to be made. Who would give the speech to the United Nations: CIA director George Tenet or Secretary of State Colin Powell? In the end, the group decided that Tenet would sit in Powell's shadow as he presented the case—providing a kind of gravitas. Powell practiced the speech several times in the cafeteria of the U.S. mission at the UN.

The speech served as high drama.[33] Powell presented graphic depictions of mobile biological weapon death machines that WINPAC analysts had drawn up. High-resolution satellite images were shown that had convinced Colonel Wilkerson and his staff that Saddam Hussein had moved chemical weapons in anticipation of UN inspections. The speech included information from the British dossier, compiled by MI6, the British foreign intelligence service. Powell showed evidence that Iraq had obtained elaborate mapping software that included maps of the eastern United States, being used by Iraq perhaps to plan an attack. Powell even held up the replication of a vial of anthrax to emphasize how a small amount of anthrax could do a large amount of harm.

Emergence of Dissenting Views

Upon hearing that Curveball's information would be used in the upcoming speech to the United Nations, the only U.S. intelligence official to meet Curveball sent a memo to the CIA outlining his concerns about the source. In reply, he received the following e-mail from the deputy of the CIA Counter Proliferation Unit:

> As I said last night, let's keep in mind the fact that this war's going to happen regardless of what Curveball said or didn't say, and the Powers that Be probably aren't terribly interested in whether Curveball knows what he's talking about. However, in the interest of Truth, we owe somebody a sentence or two of warning, if you honestly have reservations.[34]

Drumheller called Tenet in New York the night before the presentation and spoke with Tenet on the phone. He disputed the reliability of Curveball.[35] When Drumheller watched the presentation on a television monitor within the CIA, he was astounded that Powell was reciting, almost word for word, the intelligence provided by the human intelligence source Curveball. Powell's speech worked just well enough to move public opinion in the direction of war. Positive support for the invasion of Iraq jumped seven percentage points (from 50% to 57%), according to a Gallup poll.[36]

Powell delivered his speech as Wilkerson listened carefully in the hallway. Sitting directly behind Powell was CIA Director George Tenet, along with the future ambassador to Iraq, John Negroponte. Across from Powell was Jack Straw, the British foreign minister, alongside other members of the UN Security Council. For the first time Wilkerson was listening quietly to Powell's presentation.

> I realized as I watched it there in the UN Security Council, for the first time, because every time I watched it before I was running around, trying to get things changed—do this, do that, talking about the graphics and everything else. But there in the UN Security Council I sat down quietly and watched Secretary Powell make his presentation. I wouldn't go to war based on that. That's what I told myself. Most of it could be interpreted differently from the way we represented it.[37]

After the presentation, Wilkerson walked out of the UN building into the bracingly cold New York City wind. "It was a total failure," he thought to himself. Having played such an important part in putting the presentation together, he considered it his failure.

Limited Wartime Evidence to Support Belief in Iraq's Active Weapons of Mass Destruction Program

As the first battalions of U.S. troops crossed over the Kuwait border into the vast Iraqi desert, analysts sweated on what was sure to be a "tragic and bloody final act," as many had predicted. They waited as Saddam brought out his stores of chemical and biological weapons to use against U.S. troops as they marched on toward Baghdad. But, thankfully, these hits never came.

Analysts, soldiers, and politicians all took a big sigh of relief once they realized that Saddam would not be releasing his arsenal of WMD on troops as they headed for Baghdad. Even as the race to find the hidden caches of WMD went into top gear, the lack of an early attack seemed a real mystery. The major justification for war rested on the notion that active WMD programs existed, yet the first anticipated piece of evidence for WMD—that Saddam would use chemical and biological weapons during the march on Baghdad—failed to materialize. Army Major General James Marks's search of suspected WMD sites continued to come up short. But with only a limited staff, Marks could only visit a site or two per week, and at that pace, it would take years to uncover any tangible evidence of WMD.[38]

Marks and his crew worked feverishly to uncover WMD, but the politicians and bureaucrats back in Washington and on Downing Street became increasingly anxious. Nearly three months into the war, nothing had been uncovered. Tenet and others watched as the military efforts to find WMD began to get bogged down. Marks not only lacked the necessary resources to cover the sites, but he also became deeply embroiled in the bureaucracy of the military. The CIA suggested a change of tactics based on intelligence rather than a military focus. Tenet called in David Kay, a veteran weapons inspector, to move in a new direction.[39]

Kay, formerly an employee of the government contractor Science Applications International Corporation, now served as a commentator for NBC News. Kay had spent the earlier part of his career in academics. After years of serving as a high-profile weapons inspector and then working in front of the camera full time, Kay brought both the media talent and experience needed to recharge the search for WMD. A little academic mindfulness did not hurt his "street credibility" either. He looked nonpartisan, an objective source in the race to find WMD.

Kay had no doubt that Saddam stored WMD ready to fire at a moment's notice. Knowing this possibility, Kay took the search in a different direction than Marks. Kay believed the method of trying to visit each of the 946 sites was a race that he couldn't win. It represented a linear and rather thoughtless approach. Kay adopted an intelligence approach, focusing on the current information rather than specific locations of WMD stockpiles in Iraq. After years of weapons inspecting in Iraq, the U.S. and British intelligence services had a comprehensive list of Iraqi engineers, technicians, and administrators involved in weapons production.

Over the many years of weapons inspections in Iraq, the UN-led inspection teams had actually been quite effective, it turns out, in keeping Iraq on the run. Yet for all their secrecy, the Iraqis had kept detailed records of all their weapons programs. The records included comprehensive personnel files of all those who had worked on the programs. Kay's newly energized strategy to find WMD went after these individuals first. He worried about the actual sites themselves second. Kay and his team, now renamed the Iraq Survey Group (ISG), sought out people rather than places.

One of the substrategies of the ISG involved a general call to the Iraqi people for information on WMD. The ISG offered attractive sums of money in exchange for information. Informants flooded their offices. One Iraqi presented evidence of a covered-up weapons cache behind a school, whereas another pointed to a waste dump. Unfortunately, most or all of these efforts turned out to be false leads. Informants were more interested in the money than WMD.

The Search for Curveball's Identity

Some of the CIA analysts who had read information on the Curveball source with enthusiasm back in August of 2002 were now part of the ISG.[40] One primary objective of the bioweapons inspector group focused on finding information on Curveball. Being in Iraq again must have been a surreal experience. Having read about this source in an abstract way, defending his credibility, they were on a manhunt. The manhunt, however, was not for the man himself, because they knew where he was. Rather, the hunt involved a search for Curveball's identity. Did the man known as Curveball exist as he had said, or was his identity just an elaborate deception?

The inspectors visited the site that Curveball had mentioned. When in the custody of his German intelligence handlers, Curveball claimed he worked at the facility at Djerf al-Naddaf, outside of Baghdad. This is where he claimed the accident occurred that exposed him to anthrax spores. When the weapons inspector team arrived at the site, their search for the Curveball file came up empty. Such a record would include his real name, his picture, and his length of service. Without it, verification of his credentials would be virtually impossible.

As analysts, they needed more facts. In order to vet their source, they needed to see proof that Curveball had worked in the mobile laboratories. They needed a personnel file. Just as the analysts were ready to give up all hope of finding such a file, a young Iraqi approached the team with a batch of files from a related program—one not officially recognized by the Iraqis—housed in an adjacent building. Through a translator, the team learned of a secret program designed to convert agricultural seeding equipment from making seed slurry to anthrax slurry, the basis for turning anthrax into deadly weapons. They quickly whipped through the files and hit a home run: Curveball had been found!

The team rented a car and traversed Baghdad and its suburbs in a race to track down the identity of the elusive Curveball. They sought out Curveball's family and friends, as well as his neighbors and enemies. All the people they met told the same story: Curveball failed the truth test. Friends called him "a great liar" and a "con artist." When they finally found Curveball's family, his mother invited the team into their house and into his bedroom. Despite what the Germans claimed, Curveball did not hate Americans at all. In fact, his room was covered with posters of American rock stars! As surprising as this new revelation was, CIA analysts knew all too well that all they had was rumor, opinion, and word of mouth. These were the tools of operative spies. Operatives lived for this kind of information. These "softer" insights often seemed like false leads too; you could only count on them so much. As analysts they needed hard facts.

Close inspection of his file proved what Curveball's Iraqi acquaintances confirmed, that he served only as a low-level trainee engineer and he had been fired in the mid 1990s. By the time the human source known as Curveball defected to Germany, he was nothing more than a Baghdad taxi driver. Growing evidence pointed to the fact that he had simply gathered information from a variety of public sources, like the Internet, and cobbled it together with limited insights on chemical manufacturing that he had learned from his few short years at a chemical factory. His knowledge conformed quite closely to the story told in the British dossier and other documents that were a compilation of public knowledge.

Years later, Curveball exposed his identity and gave an interview for the U.S. television show *60 Minutes*.[41] Some years later, he appeared in the press again, explaining his motives as patriotic. He lied only to see Saddam the dictator over-thrown in order to set his country free. Whatever his motive, according to many sources, most of Curveball's story proved false. In the end, it appeared that most of what Curveball cited as inside information, he gathered from open-source data on Iraq WMD.[42]

In late June, analysts boarded a military transport for home, ready to take the case back to CIA headquarters at Langley. The Iraqi desert must have seemed so distant from the hectic Virginia traffic they had dodged to get to work nearly a year ago. They carried with them Curveball's personnel file, which showed that Curveball had not worked at the Djerf al-Naddaf facility during the time of the alleged accident. Contrary to what they were told by the foreign intelligence ser-vices, it appeared he admired U.S. culture. They also held Curveball's college academic transcripts. There was no evidence that he was a sought-after chemical engineer who showed great academic success; instead his transcript showed a string of "50s"; he hadn't even passed his major courses.[43]

STAGE 4: REBUILDING LEARNING

After months of data collection within the borders of the newly liberated Iraq, there were increased doubts that Iraq held an active WMD program at all. A com-prehensive survey of human intelligence sources in Iraq, hundreds of interviews with Iraqis involved in the WMD program, close inspection of multiple sus-pected sites, and detailed reading of Iraqi personnel files resulted in a dead end.[44]

Moreover, the mapping software of the eastern United States held in the hands of Iraq, which contributed to the case for Iraq, proved no more than an add-on to a plane they had bought.[45] The contractors who sold the navigation system to Iraq had added on a feature—a map used only for training pilots and operators how to use the system, no different than a simulator. Saddam had little intention of bombing the United States with WMD. Finally, those familiar with the psychology of Saddam had believed that, backed into a corner, he would have used WMD by now to slow down the advance of U.S. troops, but no such actions were taken on a grand scale.

Red Teams

By June 2003, John McLaughlin, deputy director of the CIA and one of the lead investigators on the Iraq WMD efforts within the CIA, knew something was wrong. Too much evidence began to challenge the conventional wisdom shared among most members within the organization. When the doubts set in and the need to update the organization's position was clarified, McLaughlin's chief analyst immediately set up a "red team," an external review group that would deconstruct every piece of intelligence, scrutinize it, and challenge every bit of the available information. The red team conducted a complete review of every piece of evidence that went into the October 2002 NIE, as well as the details of Powell's speech to the UN.

We might imagine what it would be like to have been an analyst within the CIA at this time and the frustration that was experienced due to the uncertainty about WMD. As McLaughlin would later say about biological WMD in Iraq, "Make no mistake, we were wrong."[46] But the public recognition of this mistake would not occur for months.[47]

With growing realization that WMD did not exist, it was with great frustration that many of those within the CIA watched as George Tenet presented his speech at Georgetown University on February 5, 2004. Now, nearly a year after the invasion, Tenet and others continued to track the search closely. There are no weapons, many inside pleaded. Tenet, barely stopping to hear the case, continued his forward motion, like a running back who just dodged a tackle and headed for the end zone. He needed to reassure an anxious public to be patient, to give the search more time, to continue to have faith. Tenet would deliver a speech about WMD that assured the audience that "as we meet here today, the Iraq Survey Group is continuing its important search for weapons, people, and data." Despite his persistence, he also confessed in the same speech that the CIA may have been wrong in some cases. He stated:

> And I must tell you we are finding discrepancies in some claims made by human sources about mobile Biological Weapons production before the war. Because we lack direct access to the most important sources on this question, we have as yet been unable to resolve the differences. My provisional bottom line today: Iraq intended to develop Biological Weapons.[48]

Many within the organization now began to realize that in assessing the original WMD threat, the threshold of truth had been set too low. The threat itself outweighed the need for absolute certainty. In assessing the fact that WMD did not exist, the threshold would need to be set high. After all, a crude biological weapon could fit into the glove compartment of a Toyota. Now the red team needed to confirm the opposite, and it was difficult to prove with certainty that WMD did not exist.

Cultural Adjustment

In the aftermath of the learning breakdown on WMD in Iraq, John McLaughlin reflected with me on how to rebuild in the face of a breakdown of learning.

We were all devastated when we found out the NIE wasn't correct. It was devastating. The only thing you can do is to stare it in the face.... You ask yourself, "What happened?" It is an extremely helpful but painful process. It is always tempting to deny your own role. You cannot permit yourself to go into denial because you are dealing with another new problem the next day. If you go into denial, you are going to go deeper and deeper. Not addressing the issues that led to the problem, digging deeper into self-denial only furthers the organization's problem. If you don't address the issues, ... you are driven to commit the same mistake again.[49]

This narrative description of an organizational experience of a breakdown in learning highlights some of the challenges discussed throughout the book faced by organizations as they learn their way through challenging situations. Whether the organization is operating in routine circumstances or novel ones, learning provides the mechanisms for uncovering lapses in learning and rebuilding resilience in organizations. The next chapter outlines specific examples of organizational breakdown, drawing from the events recounted in this chapter as well as other events presented in this book.

CONCLUSION

This chapter has presented a case study of the learning, justification, and eventual retraction associated with the U.S. intelligence community's search for biological WMD in Iraq. The chapter shows how organizational factors, such as politics, power, destructive goal pursuit, and other factors combined to threaten learning. The purpose of the chapter was to reveal how the breakdown of learning unfolds in a knowledge-based organization. The next chapter reveals how other factors, including culture, hasten the breakdown of learning and begins to identify factors that hasten the rebuilding of learning.

ENDNOTES

1. The scenario of the analysts comes from Drogin and Goetz (2005). Specifically see p. 250, where he quoted one analyst saying, "I was wrong."
2. References to "the analysts" is a reference to composite characters. For the story of a specific analyst, see "Jerry" from Drogin and Goetz (2005) and Drogin (2007).
3. This section is taken from a number of sources, including Drogin and Goetz (2005) and Drogin (2007). See also the Silberman-Robb report (Commission on the Intelligence Capabilities of the United States Regarding Weapons of Mass Destruction, 2005, pp. 193–194), and the National Public Radio story (Montagne, Butler, & Kelly, 2002).
4. The quote is from Cheney (2002).
5. The description of the analyst job came from a variety of sources. See also the Select Committee on Intelligence, U.S. Senate (2004), pp. 4–8, and Best (2005).

6. See also Johnston (2005).
7. For more on the relationship between the U.S. intelligence community and Iraq, see National Security Archive (1995–2004). See also, from a British perspective, Intelligence and Security Committee, House of Commons (2003) and U.K. Joint Intelligence Committee (2002).
8. This comes from the *Congressional Record–Senate*, October 9, 2002, p. S10154, retrieved from http://www.gpo.gov/fdsys/pkg/CREC-2002-10-09/pdf/CREC-2002-10-09-pt1-PgS10145-2.pdf#page=10. The hearing was declassified the next day.
9. For more information on perceptions of the threat posed by Saddam Hussein, see Post (2003, 2004).
10. See Post (2004), p. 223.
11. For details on biological weapons, see Laqueur (1999).
12. For details on the case for Curveball, see Commission on the Intelligence Capabilities of the United States Regarding Weapons of Mass Destruction (2005), pp. 98–99. For details on the Curveball affair, see Select Committee on Intelligence, U.S. Senate (2004), pp. 15–156, and the Commission on the Intelligence Capabilities of the United States Regarding Weapons of Mass Destruction (2005), pp. 80–111. Also see Drogin (2007). See also the segment on Curveball that appeared on *60 Minutes* (Mihailovich, 2007).
13. The quote is from the Select Committee on Intelligence, U.S. Senate (2004), p. 156.
14. For details on skeptics of Curveball, see Select Committee on Intelligence (2004), pp. 154–158.
15. The Select Committee on Intelligence (2004) recorded that a Department of Defense intelligence analyst held concerns that he "thought [Curveball] might be an alcoholic" (p. 154). The same analyst later reported that he had "concern with the validity of information based on 'Curveball' having a terrible hangover the morning…"; the remainder of the sentence was redacted (p. 154).
16. Accounts of the meeting between Drumheller and "Gradl," the German BND intelligence official, can be found in the Commission on the Intelligence Capabilities of the United States Regarding Weapons of Mass Destruction (2005), pp. 94–95. See also Drumheller (2006), pp. 79–80. In his book, Drumheller refers to his meeting with his German counterpart "Lothar" (p. 205). Here, I have referred to this German agent in terms of what appears to be his undercover name, "Gradl."
17. See Drumheller (2006), p. 82.
18. The meeting recounted appears in the Commission on the Intelligence Capabilities of the United States Regarding Weapons of Mass Destruction (2005), pp. 94–105. See also Drumheller's (2006) account of these events and *60 Minutes* (Gelber & Bach, 2006).
19. Information on Pillar and his role in compiling the NIE came primarily from an author interview (2008). See also Pillar (2003) for information on terrorism and Pillar's interview on *Frontline* (PBS, 2006). For more on the relationship between policy and intelligence, see Pillar (2006) and Best (2005).
20. Quotes in this section are from an author interview (2008).
21. For more on the early years of the CIA, see Thomas (2006).
22. For details on the pressure placed on analysts by policymakers, see Kerr, Wolfe, Donegan, and Pappas (2004).
23. Analysts discuss the role of Vice President Cheney in *The Dark Side* (PBS, 2006).
24. For an alternative view of events from Feith's perspective, see Feith (2008).
25. For Douglas Feith's presentation, see Feith (2002).
26. The quote is from the Senate's assessment of Feith's work; see Levin (2004).

27. The quote is from an author interview with Lawrence Wilkerson (2008).
28. The quote is from *60 Minutes* (Gelber & Bach, 2006).
29. For Powell's presentation to the UN, see Powell (2003).
30. For details on the government's case for Curveball, see Commission on the Intelligence Capabilities of the United States Regarding Weapons of Mass Destruction (2005), pp. 98–99. See also Central Intelligence Agency (2002) and Central Intelligence Agency and Defense Intelligence Agency (2003).
31. The quote is from an author interview with Wilkerson (2008).
32. In author interviews with each of them, McLaughlin and Wilkerson characterized the meeting as difficult and exhausting.
33. For a transcript of Powell's presentation to the UN, see Powell (2003).
34. The e-mail is from Senate Select Committee on Intelligence Report (2004), p. 249.
35. Details of the call between Tenet and Drumheller can be found in the Commission on the Intelligence Capabilities of the United States Regarding Weapons of Mass Destruction (2005), p. 104. Drumheller's personal account of these events can be found in Drumheller (2006). George Tenet and John McLaughlin both challenged Drumheller's account; see McLaughlin (2005) and Tenet (2004; 2007, pp. 376–383). See also Tenet (2002).
36. Although the poll is cited in Drumheller (2006), p. 103, his representation may be a bit misleading. The poll did show an increase in approval for the war for those who actually watched the speech, but Gallup analysts concluded the speech itself had little impact overall (Jones, 2003). For a poll of U.S. citizens months later, see Harris Interactive (2006), the Harris Poll #57.
37. Wilkerson's reaction to Powell's speech is available at Wilkerson (2007). The quote is from that interview.
38. Details about Major General James Marks come from Bob Woodward (2006), pp. 92–99.
39. For more on David Kay's experiences, see Woodward (2006), PBS (2006), and the videotaped interview in Greenwald (2004).
40. This section is based on the work of Drogin and Goetz (2005) and Drogin (2007, pp. 237–242). See also Commission on the Intelligence Capabilities of the United States Regarding Weapons of Mass Destruction (2005, pp. 193–194).
41. See *60 Minutes* (Mihailovich, 2007). See also Mihailovich (2011).
42. Drogin (2007) suggested that Curveball might have retrieved his knowledge of WMD from public sources.
43. See Drogin (2007) and *60 Minutes* (Mihailovich, 2007) for details on Curveball's academic achievements.
44. For more information on intelligence failure and the search for WMD, see the Commission on the Intelligence Capabilities of the United States Regarding Weapons of Mass Destruction (2005). This commission, in its so-called Silberman-Robb report, was tasked only with looking at the intelligence aspects and explicitly excluded consideration of policy-related activities. Thus, the Silberman-Robb report rested on a foregone conclusion. Additionally, according to Bob Woodward (2006), "Silberman considered both Cheney and Rumsfeld his close personal friends" (p. 26). Silberman swore Rumsfeld into office as secretary of defense. Silberman's wife had worked closely with Vice President Cheney's wife on political activities. When Silberman was recruited to head the commission, Cheney called Silberman and told him, "We want to have a commission to look at the intelligence community to determine whether the intelligence community properly evaluated the question of weapons of mass destruction in Iraq" (Woodward, 2006, p. 284). Despite political

and personal biases that may have guided the report, many I spoke with found the report accurate. See also the Select Committee on Intelligence, U.S. Senate (2004). Despite a comprehensive review of the intelligence and extensive interviews with intelligence officials, the report could not overcome political divides in Congress at that time. Democratic minority members concluded that the report "fails to fully explain the environment of intense pressure in which Intelligence Community officials were asked to render judgments on matters related to Iraq when policy officials had already forcefully stated their own conclusions in public" (p. 449). For an alternative view from either the President's Commission or the Senate Commission reports, see the CIA's internal review (Kerr et al., 2004). See also Committee of Privy Counsellors (2004) (Butler Review) for a review of the intelligence from the U.K. perspective.

45. The mapping software problem was discussed by Wilkerson on *Frontline* (PBS, 2006).
46. The McLaughlin (2008a) quote is from a George Washington University presentation. Information on the red team also came from this presentation.
47. See Special Advisor to the Director of Central Intelligence on Iraq's Weapons of Mass Destruction (2005).
48. The Tenet quote is from Tenet (2004).
49. Author interview (McLaughlin, 2008b).

CHAPTER 10

Revisiting the Universal Dilemma of Learning in Policy, Government, and Organizational Culture

The previous chapter explored how learning broke down in the U.S. intelligence community. The breakdown in intelligence is best explored in the context of other policy-related breakdowns such as the Challenger launch decision and the Kennedy administration in light of the Bay of Pigs fiasco. The chapter begins with a look at learning in the financial services industry.

Lloyd Blankfein served as CEO and president of Goldman Sachs, perhaps the world's best-known investment bank in 2008. He was asked to reflect on the global banking crisis and if he thought such a catastrophic event could happen again. Blankfein reflected on the collapse of Goldman Sachs's two major competitors, Lehman Brothers and Bear Stearns. He responded by asserting his belief in the importance of being prepared for even the worst scenarios. Low-probability events, such as the market crash, will happen, he said, while expressing little doubt that organizations need to be prepared for anything, especially those events they can't predict (Holliday, 2013). Blankfein spoke with the confidence he acquired from experience that was itself derived from learning. Earlier in the book, I outlined the definition of experience offered by philosopher Richard Palmer. It is worth repeating: "It is the 'experienced' [person] who knows the limitations of all anticipation, the insecurity of all human plans. Yet this does not render [that person] rigid and dogmatic but rather open for new experience.... Experience teaches the incompleteness of all plans" (Palmer, 1969, p. 196). Palmer the philosopher seems to share with Blankfein the banker a belief that to acknowledge the incompleteness of knowledge—acknowledging the possibility of novelty and being prepared to respond to novel situations—is a key to learning. This is the knowledge gained from experience. Both philosopher and business leader reflect one of the primary themes of this book: appreciation for uncertainty acquired through experience and the importance of learning from experience as the basis of organizational knowledge.

Wilensky (1967) called the inability to learn from experience one of the fundamental dilemmas of organizational life. All organizations face the fundamental dilemma of learning from experience as they seek the accurate, timely, and useful interpretation of information. Inflexibility, an inability to adapt, an overemphasis on performance at the expense of learning, reliance on rational decision making, and narrow definitions of what constitutes success conspire to undermine learning in the contemporary organization. A refusal or inability to acknowledge how political agendas shape learning creates additional dilemmas. The question then becomes how to build learning from experience and the notion that anything can happen in organizational practices. A review of research and practice suggests opportunities for future learning in this regard.

THE SEARCH FOR WEAPONS OF MASS DESTRUCTION AS MIDEDUCATIVE EXPERIENCES

Chapter 2 discussed how consensus is an important determinant of how and what is learned in organizations. Government provides an interesting example of the barriers to learning that may arise from low consensus. Organizations that lack consensus lack a prerequisite for learning (Fiol, 1994), which leads to miseducative experiences. The race for weapons of mass destruction (WMD) and other events recounted throughout the book reveal how low-consensus organizations can lead to miseducative experiences.

Miseducative experiences occur when organizations repeat old mistakes and habits rather than develop new ones that prove more adaptive. For example, archival data suggest that the U.S. intelligence community engaged in a string of overestimations on the weapons capability of the Soviet Union during the Cold War. The dominant assumption that Russia posed a strategic and tactical threat persisted until former Soviet-bloc nations declared their independence in 1991. Similarly with Iraq, the intelligence had relied heavily on outdated information. In 1991, the intelligence community had been shocked to find the capabilities that Iraq had amassed. They relied on this same information and assessment in the race for WMD more than a decade later.

Another type of miseducative experience emerges when conclusions that are already held become further reinforced. Analysis of the search for WMD suggests that the intelligence community sought to reinforce the belief that Iraq held and was continuing programs for WMD. This conclusion emerged after several miscalculations over Iraq's capabilities, beginning in 1991 when it was discovered that Iraq had come within a year of developing nuclear capability, and again in the mid 1990s after inspectors were surprised that Iraq had continued experiments to weaponize chemical and biological material. Thus, the intelligence community had decided "to set the bar low." In other words, unless there was significant intelligence to the contrary, the default position was to reinforce existing beliefs about the existence of WMD. At other times, beliefs may become hardened rather than flexible. The continued reinforcement of existing conclusions only serves to solidify existing beliefs. Beliefs are held solely by individuals, whereas institutions adopt beliefs in the form of doctrine, assumptions, and protocol. Analysis of documents relating to Iraq and WMD reveals that institutionalized forces were also at work.

The story of Jerry, the Central Intelligence Agency (CIA) analyst who at one time strongly supported the belief that Iraq had a continuing WMD program, demonstrates how organizational beliefs may become hardened over time. After visiting Iraq several times and working in the Iraq Survey Group, a multinational task force of more than 1,000 inspectors who combed Iraq for WMD, Jerry concluded that WMD did not exist and that one of the key sources, Curveball, was a fraud. When Jerry returned to CIA headquarters, he endured much stress and was eventually ostracized from his division for questioning the beliefs of the organization. One report claimed he became a "non-person" (Drogin, 2007).

A third type of miseducative experience occurs when evidence is used simply to confirm rather than test or develop a belief. One of the effects of goal setting is the propensity to confirm existing beliefs rather than inspire testing or development of new beliefs. The notion, stated publicly by officials, that Iraq had WMD became official policy. In line with this official policy, all existing and incoming information served to confirm the existing goal of finding WMD. Some sources cited officials making private comments about WMD as early as September 2001. By August 2002, the notion that Iraq had WMD became public. The important question shifted: It was no longer, "Does Iraq have WMD?" but rather, "What information can be used publicly in support of the fact that Iraq has WMD?"

One of the most common miseducative experiences in organizations occurs when individuals miss the complexity of situations, including their richness and detail. Finally, and most vividly, goal setting leads to an elimination of situation complexity, including the richness, details, and contingencies necessary for the nuanced work of intelligence. If organizations themselves serve as a means to simplify complexity, then goal setting forms the justification for such simplification. Several specific institutional attempts occurred to simplify the relevant data to fit the simple and direct goal of finding WMD. One example was the use of ad hoc teams, such as the Center for Weapons Intelligence, Nonproliferation, and Arms Control (WINPAC) analysis team. WINPAC was developed as a means of bypassing bureaucratic processes to get information regarding Iraq directly to the CIA director's office. Bypassing traditional filtering channels in the bureaucracy made information more accessible, but it also resulted in information being selected that fit the original goal.

Miseducative experiences in the intelligence community serve as cautionary tales to understand the consequences that ensue when organizations require conformity to a rigid goal. Old assumptions are not questioned, new and competing information becomes hard to integrate, and challenges to the prevailing cultural beliefs get lost. Leaders often risk falling into the procrustean formula as they try to overcome the competing loyalties of followers. When leaders rely primarily on performance mode, critical thinking and learning are sacrificed.

LEARNING FROM POLICY FIASCOS

To more fully explore the search for WMD is to consider it within the context of two other fiascos: the Bay of Pigs invasion and the Cuban missile crisis. The Bay of Pigs invasion, which occurred in April 1961, was an unsuccessful military invasion of Cuba intended to overthrow the revolutionary government of Fidel Castro. The invading force was defeated by Cuban armed forces within three days. The Cuban missile crisis occurred 18 months later. This 13-day confrontation, which involved the United States in discussions with Cuba and the Soviet Union, succeeded in averting a nuclear conflict. These two events are well known and have been the subject of organizational analysis for nearly half a century. Scholars have gone to great lengths to study them, usually considering the events in the context of organizational decision making, the psychology of groups, or as historical events. What has been missing is a study of these events from the perspective of learning and its breakdown.

The Cuban missile crisis parallels the search for WMD in several ways. Both cases represent how organizations overcome the challenges of learning, what Wilensky called "universal dilemmas of organizational life." Allison and Zelikow (1999) argued that the ultimate assessment of the CIA in the Cuban missile crisis may have been wrong, but the decisions made were not ill informed. From Allison and Zelikow's viewpoint, the Cuban missile crisis reveals a picture of the tremendous promise that learning offers and the remarkable ability displayed by contemporary organizations to grasp complex forms of information. Despite all the obstacles, challenges, anxieties, and other threats to learning that loom, those in organizations demonstrate a remarkable ability to learn.

In some not-so-obvious ways, presidential cabinets, intelligence organizations, and aerospace organizations share some common characteristics that make them exemplars for studying learning. They are organizations whose primary objective lies in gathering, processing, interpreting, and communicating information (Wilensky, 1967, p. viii). They also share some characteristics of high-reliability organizations. For example, intelligence, aerospace, and executive organizations rely on a series of highly interrelated actions, activities, and beliefs that can lead to disaster when these actions are poorly coordinated (Perrow, 1999). The

U.S. intelligence community, in particular, provide an interesting environment in which to explore these factors because the intelligence community operates in a highly politicized environment, as Orton (2000) demonstrated in his analysis of the reorganization of the intelligence community under the presidency of Gerald Ford.

The Bay of Pigs invasion, the Cuban missile crisis, and the search for WMD offer a unique look at learning. Psychologist Irving Janis made a compelling observation about the role of learning in his analysis of the Cuban missile crisis. He noted that the Kennedy administration learned important lessons from the loss of lives and the ultimate failure of the invasion of Cuba in the Bay of Pigs. What he learned from the failure, according to Janis, helped lead to the successful resolution of the Cuban missile crisis. The failure of the Bay of Pigs invasion provided an experience that proved "educative" for Kennedy and his advisors. This failure created a new perspective that allowed him to successfully navigate the harrowing 13 days that would define his presidency.

The U.S. intelligence community provides an example of how organizations learn from breakdown as well. In the case of Iraq, a "red team"—a specialized team designed to conduct a complete critique of intelligence—was employed after the mission. The critique was conducted only after significant evidence pointed to a false-positive finding: that Iraq did not have WMD. In the search and destroy of Osama Bin Laden by U.S. special forces in Pakistan, the intelligence community conducted three red teams prior to the assault (Bowen, 2012). The use of red teams to challenge assumptions and offer multiple perspectives has become pervasive. Integration of various perspectives, including those with different expertise and functions, has become more common.

The comparison between the Bay of Pigs and the subsequent Cuban missile crisis and the search for WMD also has limits. After all, the 1960s Cold War operational context was characterized by a common enemy, a clear outcome, and clarity and agreement over goals. In contrast, the search for biological WMD in Iraq and many of the other events explored in this book represent the demands of contemporary organizations. If Wilensky thought complexity within organizations could fuel the breakdown of learning, he would likely be surprised at the level of complexity in the post–Cold War ear. In Eichenwald's (2012a) book, *500 Days*, he outlined the complexities of organizing and executing the Iraq war, with its web of intelligence, political, military, and diplomatic interests. The demands faced by contemporary organizations seem to pose an almost insurmountable challenge to learning.

The legacy of the WMD fiasco runs deep. *Foreign Policy* (2011) magazine reported that by 2011, eight years after the fiasco, more than 1,200 U.S. agencies were engaged in some intelligence gathering, processing, and operational activities, and the sprawling intelligence–industrial complex of private intelligence contractors has further complicated intelligence efforts (Priest & Arkin, 2010). Yet, learning continues, despite these complications.

No discussion of learning in organizations would be complete without a serious consideration of how deception, politics, and culture shape learning. Politics—the fight for power, influence, and resources—is of particular interest because it shapes how knowledge is interpreted and which interpretations receive legitimacy within the organization. Although factors such as deception, politics, and dysfunctional culture threaten to shape organizations, resilient organizations find ways to overcome these limitations.

Politics and power constitute an important part of learning and are ingrained in the learning process (Vince, 2001). Vince argued that an understanding of power and politics allows those in organizations to take a critical stance in approaching how power shapes learning and action in organizations. For example, an understanding of power might shed light on why a subordinate might be reluctant to bring bad news or share critical information that might be perceived as negative (Vince, 2001, p. 1331). Vince went so far as to argue that it would be difficult to understand what is actually learned in an organization without reference to power relations and how human interaction shapes knowledge.

The NASA Challenger launch reveals the underlying politics inherent in organizational learning. Vaughn conducted a detailed analysis of NASA. She argued that a significant factor in the decision to launch the Challenger was political pressures. She pointed to a "get the job done at any cost" culture that had emerged within NASA. The culture is reminiscent of the performance goal–directed culture that existed in NASA during the early Apollo missions, which came to be known as the "goal fever" culture. External political pressures surely played a part in both the Challenger and the Apollo breakdowns, but perhaps even more influential was the collective action and the internal narrative that had developed within NASA. The cultural narrative turned on a shared belief that the future survival of the organization was in danger if it didn't launch the Challenger space shuttle.

Another interesting example of how culture and politics shape learning was revealed in an interview I conducted with former CIA analyst Dr. Paul Pillar. He described how politics can slowly seep into intelligence analysis. Pillar played a key role in compiling the *National Intelligence Estimate: Iraq's Continuing Programs for Weapons of Mass Destruction*. I asked him how deception and self-deception can play a role in how intelligence is interpreted. Pillar responded by suggesting that deception is an attempt to create an impression that is incorrect, but deception isn't always intentional. One example of deception that he believed emerged during the review of intelligence on WMD in Iraq occurred because some stakeholders tried to create a link between Saddam Hussein and the al Qaeda terrorist network. This type of deception, he noted, "is rhetorically woven in a way that is not only false, but often contrary to the intelligence. It often involves making a certain kind of impression and it creeps into things in countless different ways" (Pillar, 2008).

Pillar noted two types of deception that might have played a part in fueling the race for WMD: public deception and private deception. In general, public deception involves the use of intelligence to convince or persuade the general public or a subset of the public to take a particular position. For example, some analysts believed that policymakers, the end users of intelligence, along with those in their sphere of influence, went on a hunt to find intelligence that solidified a connection between al Qaeda and Hussein. In this way, intelligence served not to inform a decision, but rather to substantiate an existing case in order to influence public opinion.

Private deception, on the other hand, occurs outside of the public eye. One example of this came in the form of the subtle pressure exerted by policymakers and policy influencers on members of the intelligence community to find more and better details on WMD in Iraq. As Pillar (2008) noted, "We [the CIA] would provide information, intelligence, and then it would be worded a certain way that made it look like something it wasn't." Pillar also recognized another kind of deception, self-deception, especially on the part of policymakers and other consumers of intelligence. In particular, he believed that many people can easily deceive themselves into seeing intelligence in a certain way. He explained how policymakers might spin a web of self-deception.

> First, you get policymakers starting to ask questions, asking for specific information or specific kinds of information. Next, they start seeing these details in the report regularly. Then they start thinking, "Hey, if these things are in the report, then they must be important," and they kind of forget that they asked for them to be there in the first place. When the daily flow of information is in a certain direction, you tend to see it in a certain way.
>
> (Pillar, 2008)

Deception and self-deception present a problem for those in organizations attempting to build learning into daily routines. Learning can easily become derailed as factions within an organization struggle over interpretations of data or struggle to shift attention to certain details. The lesson here suggests that learning in organizations requires constant attention to politics and power. Even though Wilensky's view of organizational intelligence considered power and politics, he largely relegated its importance to how hierarchy shapes organizations. He focused on how information becomes distorted as it moves up an organizational chain of command. In the end, accuracy becomes the victim as information wanders through organizational processes, becoming more distorted with each layer.

Culture is another important consideration in learning and its breakdown. The role of culture is linked to organizational breakdown through the work of Turner, who zeroed in on cultural shifts as a way to understand organizational breakdown. He gave, unfortunately, only limited attention to the role of politics as an element of culture. Vaughn (1996) began to fill in the gaps left by Turner in her analysis of NASA's culture and the decisions that led to the Challenger space shuttle launch. Like many cases in which learning breaks down, she concluded that it was difficult to identify any specific actions that led to the launch disaster. The breakdown resulted not from a single misjudgment, but rather from systematic decision-making processes that had developed over years. A performance orientation had become embedded in the organizational culture, and those in the organization were unable to learn. The Montparnasse train derailment, the crash of Air France Flight 447, the Standard Oil fire (discussed in the next chapter), the 4-h standard of emergency medicine, and the collapse of Enron share with NASA a preoccupation with performance at the expense of learning. Cultures such as these, in which rational decision making, formal goal setting, and optimism serve as the dominant forms of legitimation, tend to lack the foundation for learning and, therefore, foster miseducative and noneducative experiences.

The contemporary intelligence world may suffer from some of the same cultural limitations as these other organizations. Trained as an anthropologist, Dr. Robert Johnston found himself conducting one of the most comprehensive unclassified investigations on the U.S. intelligence community. Popular culture often imagines that anthropologists focus their skills of observation on indigenous people located in remote areas of the globe, seeking out the hidden dynamics of people cut off from the clatter of contemporary Western culture. Johnston, however, set his observation power on a different kind of culture: the CIA. He interviewed, observed, and surveyed analysts throughout the CIA.

One observation he made points to a broader problem encountered in organizations that threatens learning: the short-term performance orientation. A short-term orientation focuses the organization on factors that have an immediate consequence but may threaten its survival. The same short-term orientation may also lead to dysfunctional behavior when an organization is faced with novel demands.

Whether the need is to meet quarterly earnings targets or respond to a 24-hour news cycle, a short-term orientation permeates the culture of contemporary organizations. Dr. Johnston's study revealed that the same short-term focus found in business and the media has also crawled into the intelligence community. He identified that the CIA is an organization increasingly focused on short-term priorities. Many of the analysts he interviewed reported increasing pressure to meet short-term performance goals. One analyst described it this way, "I'm so busy putting out fires, I don't have any time to think about what kind of catastrophe is in store for me a month from now." Another analyst likened the work to "cramming for finals" except that it had to be done every day. Other analysts talked about being "reactive" and the need for "current production" and the pressure to report on "current events."

Many analysts felt the same pressure to meet short-term objectives when compiling the intelligence on WMD in Iraq. In prior years, compiling a National Intelligence Estimate (NIE) took months, or in some cases years, to complete. Policymakers had either ignored or were ignorant of the time required to compile a real NIE and requested that an NIE be provided within days.

In general, an NIE involves gathering individual bits of data from across the intelligence agency, aggregating disparate and divergent pieces of information collected by different sources, and is held independent of others in the organization. The CIA is, of course, the ultimate siloed organization. In many instances, compiling an NIE results in a more complete intelligence picture. As pieces of information that were once viewed only in isolation by a few individuals emerge into a document in which analysts can see the information in a broader context, a more complete picture emerges. A typical NIE involves not only organizing data, but also making judgments about its credibility, and a final NIE promises the most complete intelligence picture ever compiled about a specific country or subject.

Compiling the NIE reflects most or all of the challenges to intelligence that Wilensky (1967) outlined. These challenges include creating a picture that is "clear, timely, reliable, valid, adequate and wide ranging" (p. 121). In the case of compiling the Iraq NIE, all the same challenges existed, but the time frame for compiling the NIE was shorter than usual.

Time pressures continued. When Powell and Wilkerson requested more time to put together their presentation to the United Nations, they were told the timetable had already been set and that they would not receive more time to scrutinize the data. These time pressures, from a learning perspective, often favor the obvious over the unintended. The short-term focus lures individuals into identifying only those things that are predictable and simplistic. The focus on those aspects of a situation that are obvious and actionable may be desirable in a crisis situation, but in a situation involving deep analysis, such a focus results in a superficial understanding of a situation.

Johnston's study of the CIA revealed another important aspect of culture in the intelligence community that may have limited learning. He noticed a strong cultural preference for the simple over the complex. In a complex environment, in which information is in constant flux, loyalty to short-term needs often results in ignoring details. Only those items that are actionable surface as important. The dominant metaphor for the job of an analyst was that of a reporter, hitting the daily beat and measuring production by number of bullet points, not number of paragraphs. As one analyst said, "To understand what I do, imagine *USA Today* with spies: bullet points, short paragraphs, an occasional picture ... short and simple." Another quipped, "I've got 15 people trying to change my work into bullet points." Still others stated the reporter metaphor more directly—"Analyst is shorthand for reporter"—and commented on the lack of motivation, "It's hard to take pride in one paragraph." One voice noted, "I'm not a reporter, and I'm not a scholar, I'm somewhere in between." The culture of simplicity also seemed to permeate policymakers. The rushed NIE demanded by the U.S. Congress was read by only a handful of senators; we know this because few senators signed up to read the top-secret document. Many of those who did sign up admitted to only reading the executive summary, which set out the case for WMD but gave no dissenting opinions. Dissenting opinions appeared only in the body of the report in a limited way, mostly in the footnotes.

CONCLUSION

This chapter has provided insight into some of the factors that limit learning in organizations involved in policy and government. A short-term focus, time pressures, political pressures, and a culture of performance and action rather than learning and deep understanding threaten to limit learning. The intelligence missteps that contributed to the Iraq War offer new insights into learning in government and policy when considered within the context of well-studied policy fiascos such as the Bay of Pigs invasion, the Cuban missile crisis, and the Challenger launch decision.

CHAPTER 11
Building Learning in Organizations

The conclusion outlines experiential, organizational, and institutional mechanisms that promote learning in organizations. Although this book has focused mainly on the processes and mechanisms whereby learning breaks down, I want to end this discussion with a consideration of why organizations learn—and how organizations can maintain resilience in the face of crisis, disaster, and breakdown. Two industries are the focus of how learning leads to resilience: commercial aviation in the U.S. and the oil and gas industry.

One place to look at how to build learning can be found in the study of surgical teams conducted by Reagans, Argote, and Brooks (2005), explained in chapter 1. By rotating inexperienced team members in with more experienced team members, inexperienced individuals would not harm team process but provided needed relief in high-pressure systems while providing depth and breadth to operations.

The studies in this book reveal the natural tensions between accountability and openness to learning from experience (Morris & Moore, 2000). Some level of accountability is necessary for learning, but too much or the wrong kind of accountability can threaten learning. Morris and Moore recommended several ways to resolve this tension productively, including designating outside evaluators to set and assess standards on an industrywide basis, and creating and maintaining collaborative forums in which individuals can share experiences that serve as the basis for others to learn.

One example of efforts to improve learning from experience can be found in risk awareness practices developed by an informal group of backcountry skiers. Their initiative to increase avalanche awareness was sparked, in part, by a series of accidents in which experienced skiers were killed by an avalanche. Because no formal regulatory bodies and no formal institutional mechanisms exist to promote risk awareness in this setting, this informal group of skiers took the lead. This group, called Sportgevity, set up a website and worked to increase awareness

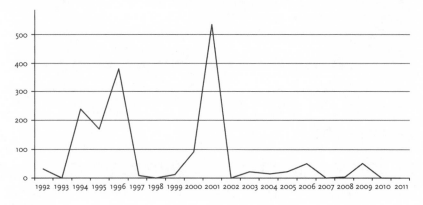

Figure 11.1:
U.S. commercial airline fatalities from 1992 to 2011.

among those who ski in backcountry environments through meetings, Internet videos, and informal communities of practice. Sportgevity is working to create a culture shift in backcountry sports that focuses on long-term sustainability and safety.

La Port's (2012) observation that learning plays an important role in understanding high-reliability organizations indicates that learning may offer ways to improve resilience in organizations. His review of the U.S. air traffic control system demonstrates how learning plays a key role in building day-to-day organizational resilience. From a statistical standpoint, there are few safer activities than flying and no safer route to one's destination than through commercial airlines. Fatal accidents are rare (Figure 11.1). Using statistics provided by the U.S. National Transportation Safety Board (2012), I estimated that if I flew on every commercial flight on a U.S.-based carrier between 1992 and 2011, my chance of being in a fatal accident was only 0.00004%. A dedication to learning, as evidenced by constant improvements in technology, development, and adherence to strong safety standards, and a culture associated with the systematic and rigorous capturing, reporting, analyzing, and correcting of errors has made incidents like the Air France 447 crash discussed in chapter 3 unlikely.

LEARNING IN COMMERCIAL AVIATION

Researchers have identified various factors that account for both failure and success in commercial aviation. Sears (1985), for example, conducted a notable review of behavioral factors associated with failures in commercial aviation. He reviewed 93 major international airline accidents between 1959 and 1983 and sought to classify the causes of those errors. Some of the major behavioral causes of accidents included pilot deviation from basic operational procedures, inadequate cross-checks by a second crew member, captains ignoring crew input, and deficiencies in communication between air traffic control and cockpit crews.

On the surface, it may seem that behavioral factors account for a significant number of aviation failures, but what researchers often overlook is that behavioral factors also account for much of the success of commercial aviation safety. Todd La Porte conducted an in-depth analysis of the air traffic control system in the 1980s (La Porte, 1988). His research on the history of the U.S. air traffic control system offers critical insights into how organizations and those inside them learn from experience. LaPorte's description of the commercial air travel system in the United States prompts the question as to why air travel can be at once one of the safest systems in the world and also one of the most complex systems that has ever existed. The success of the system depends on a unique mix of coordination and cooperation across thousands of miles, involving thousands of individual tasks that are carried out by a diverse group of operators, including pilots, regulators, engineers, designers and manufacturers, repair crews, air traffic controllers, and others. LaPorte concluded that effective operations require a constant stream of information sharing, perspective updating, openness to new information, and action taking. In other words, the success of air traffic relies to a large degree on learning. For learning to occur, the system must operate in an open environment in which processes, lessons learned, and operational details can be observed, understood, and analyzed. Even error rates, failures, and other "problems" become available as a source of public scrutiny. Learning occurs because the system is open to capturing and reporting information on both failures and successes. Although it is tempting to consider the processes associated with aviation success as cognitive sensemaking, human factors, mental models, or another facet of organizational functioning, it is essential to consider learning processes as well(see Lerner & Tetlock, 1999).

Learning is a critical success factor in commercial aviation because learning practices have been built into the technical development of the air traffic control system. For example, as new technology was introduced into the air traffic system and operations switched from manual observation and coordination of air traffic to a more technologically based system, parallel manual systems were also maintained and run in parallel with the new technology (La Porte, 1988, pp. 231–232). From a learning perspective, this parallel path had a collateral learning effect, as it allowed individuals to maintain existing routines while at the same time developing new ones.

La Porte's description of the U.S. air traffic control systems gets at something else that is often missed in studies of organizational breakdown. Many studies of organizational breakdown treat learning as if it existed in a kind of suspended animation. The studies treat learning as a constant rather than something that has emerged over time and become embedded in an organization's culture. These studies fail to tell us how organizations emerged and how their processes came about in the first place. La Porte's study started somewhere different. It started with a problem: the growing demand for passenger air travel, concerns over safety, and the threats that political infighting might derail funding. La Porte reminds us that commercial aviation did not emerge in an ideal environment. Diverse interests and interest groups resulted in continual negotiation between safety and reliability on one hand and efficiency and cost on the other. The system has always been subject to rigorous oversight by those who funded the project, those who set its policies, and the direct users. La Porte described how members of Congress, the original funding source for the expansion of commercial passenger aviation, were one of the first to see the benefits of the expanded commercial aviation system. At the same time, passengers of the system had high expectations for the system in terms of reliability and safety.

A culture built on psychological safety is central to the success of enterprises like commercial aviation. When a culture of psychological safety is built, individuals contribute lessons learned for purposes of learning rather than to avoid punishment or retaliation. The difference is a culture built on learning versus surveillance. In cultures with low psychological safety, individuals don't feel "safe" in challenging the dominant viewpoint of the organization. A culture focused on compliance rather than learning is built not on improvement, but on compliance out of a fear of retaliation. Amy Edmondson (1999) showed the systematic value of psychological safety in various organizations, including hospitals. When a culture is low in psychological safety, individuals are more likely to engage in face-saving behaviors. Face-saving behaviors are efforts put forth by an individual or group to maintain dignity, prestige, or a sense of self-worth, even when the individual or group makes a clear mistake or engages in a transgression. Face-saving behavior is largely psychological but has associated behaviors such as the propensity to ignore disconfirming data, make excuses for failures, or only look at the positive side of a problem.

The emphasis on learning in commercial aviation is also demonstrated by its gathering and analysis of information about technological and systemic breakdown. Publication of safety results, whether voluntarily or through mandate, ensures that near-miss experiences, counter experiences, and direct evidence are available for learning. One example of a publicly available source of learning is the Federal Aviation Administration's Aviation Safety Information Analysis and Sharing (ASIAS) System. Like the best organizational learning efforts, the ASIAS system captures lessons and makes them available to the general public. The site captures, codifies, and offers general theories about the nature and causes of accidents and offers insights into how to prevent them in the future by drawing on more than 40 years of government documents. The site breaks down lapses in safety into four categories: technological and human factors account for 29% of incidents; human error, 39%; crew resource management issues, such as poor leadership, poor teamwork, or interpersonal dynamics, 17%; and flight deck layout or human technology interaction and confusion, 10% (Federal Aviation

Administration, 2012; for a similar approach in the nuclear power industry, see Kerwin, Balsa, & Taylor-Adams, 1997).

LEARNING IN THE OIL AND GAS INDUSTRY

Alfred Hayes arrived in Indiana in 1930, during the height of the Depression. A chemical engineer by training, Hayes would become the assistant manager at Standard Oil of Indiana, located about 30 miles south of Chicago. He worked at Standard Oil for 50 years. An accident at the refinery where he was assistant manager rocked the city of Whiting, where the refinery was located, and foretold of an oil and gas industry in which learning would play an important role in the years to come.

Hayes helped oversee the installation of a new machine, a hydroformer, to replace aging equipment that had been installed at the plant during World War II. The new hydroformer provided the most efficient way to produce high-octane gasoline by adding a chemical mixture to unrefined oil. As Hayes and his colleagues put the machine back into production after a routine shutdown, they had no idea about the inferno that was about to erupt.

A leaky valve went undetected. The leak allowed air to circulate throughout the hydroformer. The air mixed with chemicals and gasoline already circulating through the system, and an unsafe pressure began to build up. The pressure continued to build and the valve designed to release this pressure also failed. In most cases, this wouldn't have been a problem, because the pressure could be released manually. However, the team of workers monitoring the system didn't realize that the pressure gauge, which would have reported the high pressure, had failed as well. Thus, the workers were unable to accurately assess the growing pressure inside the machine, and pressure continued to build up unnoticed.

Over the next few hours, a highly flammable material had developed inside the hydroformer completely undetected by the crew. Accident investigators could not pinpoint the exact location of the ignition, but noted that the explosion it triggered blew through a two and a half–inch think wall of the hydroformer and that 600 pieces of the hydroformer's wall were turned into shrapnel that blew up to a mile away. The shrapnel pierced nearby oil and gas storage tanks, which immediately caught fire. Fire crews brought in sand and cold water to contain the fire, which raged on for eight days (Advance Research, 1965).

In the 30 years afterward, Standard Oil of Indiana would publish 10 safety manuals directly addressing oil refinery safety. The manuals address some of the problems that led to the 1955 fire: the failure to monitor, detect, and correct the emerging problems that led to a system breakdown. The 1955 Standard Oil fire illustrates the challenges of learning in organizations and reveals how, despite breakdown, organizations can rebuild learning even in highly volatile circumstances.

What was Standard Oil in 1955 is now part of BP, a large conglomerate involved in every aspect of extracting, refining, and selling oil and gas. Sixty years after the Standard Oil Fire in Whiting, Indiana, BP experienced another operational disaster. On March 23, 2005, more than 170 workers were injured and 15 killed in an explosion at BP's Texas City plant. The site had already experienced a fatal breakdown in 2004, and two more incidents would occur in the summer of 2005. Unlike the Standard Oil accident of 1955, which observers attributed primarily to technical and engineering breakdowns, the incident as Texas City could not be tracked to specific engineering failures. The breakdown that occurred in BP's Texas City plant was largely attributed to cultural and organizational factors. According to the formal report issued by BP's internal investigation of the incident at Texas City (Mogford, 2005), several organizational factors contributed to the breakdown.

Members of the Mogford panel, charged with reviewing the accident, expressed particular concern about the organization's culture. The panel reported that the culture of the organization had eroded and this led to a loss of trust between front-line employees and managers. The result was that employees lacked motivation and purpose, rules were ignored, and employees no longer felt they had control over safety or other organizational functions. A breakdown in the learning culture arose from a systematic breakdown in safety operations, as risk management was not seen as a priority. In fact, employees became complacent and began to accept levels of risk that would have been deemed unacceptable at other BP plants and were no longer acceptable by industry standards. In other words, employees displayed low levels of "hazard awareness."

The complex nature of the organization's operations also contributed to the breakdown. The complexity in the organization and management's inability to deal with the complexity led to confusion, poor communication, and role ambiguity. Finally, communication between front-line workers and managers, what the report referred to as "vertical communication," also broke down. The result was that many of the early warning signs of pending breakdown were not communicated and front-line employees failed to push concerns or observations through the chain of command.

Underlying the culture that contributed to the breakdown, the report cited a lack of leadership. The report reviewed documents and conducted interviews with employees throughout the company, concluding that leadership lay at the heart of the breakdown. The report noted:

> BP has not adequately established process safety as a core value across its U.S. refineries. The Panel believes that a primary reason that process safety is not more widely shared as a core value in the U.S. refinery workforce is that BP executive and corporate refining management have not provided effective process safety leadership. Instead, they provided the refining workforce with a plethora of messages concerning many values, and these tended to dilute the importance of any corporate vision on

safety generally, much less process safety in particular. As discussed below, the Panel believes that BP has not provided effective leadership on or established appropriate operational expectations regarding process safety performance at its U.S. refineries. The Panel also believes that the lack of effective leadership was systemic, touching all levels of BP's corporate management having responsibilities relating to BP's U.S. refineries.

Mogford, 2005, p. 600

BP's own analysis of the disaster reveals an underlying culture that lacked a commitment to learning and a leadership team that paid too little attention to systematic safety concerns. The report concluded that BP had

> mistakenly used improving personal safety performance (i.e., personal injury rates) as an indication of acceptable process safety performance at its five U.S. refineries; BP's reliance on this data and inadequate process safety understanding created a false sense of confidence that it was properly addressing process safety risks at those refineries. (p. 72)

While BP was focusing on individual safety, managers continued to overestimate the actual safety of the system itself as they continued to miss inspections, overlook warning signs, and fail to track and address minor issues that could spiral into larger problems. When problems were tracked, there was little follow up, as no one was directly responsible for ensuring safety (p. 217; see also p. 94).

At BP, rebuilding its capacity to learn in the face of breakdown was deemed so important that an independent panel was commissioned to study the incident and make recommendations for improving operations and operational safety. The independent panel, known as the "Baker Panel" (2007) named after the commission's chair, former U.S. Secretary of State James Baker, came to similar conclusions as BP's internal investigation, the Mogford Commission. The Baker Panel offered several recommendations to improve safety at BP.

1. Improve process safety leadership. Leaders within the company needed to define effective safety processes and demonstrate commitment to maintaining those processes across the organization, including developing policies and a culture that supported the value of safety.
2. Develop an integrated and comprehensive process safety management system. The organization needed to build an integrated management system to identify, track, and ultimately reduce risks across its portfolio of operations. This would be accomplished by conducting a series of audits and reviews and tracking near-misses, accidents, and early warning signs through inspections.
3. Improve safety and knowledge expertise. Employees at all levels should understand system-related safety as well as individual safety measures.

4. Build a culture of trust and psychological safety. The organization and its leaders needed to build a culture that promoted positive and trusting relationships, in particular a culture where issues and concerns about safety and operations could be openly discussed.

5. Set expectations of accountability for managers and support for line managers. Responsibility and accountability for specific safety measures needed to be identified. Line management would be provided with better resources, training, and other types of support.

6. Identify indicators for systemic performance, not just individual performance. The organization needed to identify, implement, and update industry standards for measuring safety and production performance. Trade groups, external consultants, and professional continuity planners would be enlisted in this effort.

7. Accountability needed to start at the highest levels, beginning with the board of directors. All of these recommendations needed to be implemented and monitored at the highest level in the organization to ensure accountability for all members.

The recommendations offered by both internal and external evaluators of the BP Texas City incident track similar changes made throughout the industry, but not yet adopted by BP's Texas City plant. It's not clear if these recommendations were implemented; however, in April 2010, BP experienced another learning breakdown when its offshore drilling platform, the Deepwater Horizon, experienced a malfunction and spilled tons of oil into the Gulf of Mexico. The accident resulted in 11 deaths, and billions of dollars in lawsuits emerged.

ExxonMobil, another oil and gas company, had experienced its own high-profile breakdown in March of 1989, when one of its oil tanker ships crashed and spilled an estimated 240,000 barrels of oil in the Bligh Reef off the coast of Alaska. The company had eliminated nearly 40% of its workforce the year before in order to cut costs. Exxon seems to have taken a different direction than some of its competitors in terms of safety. The Exxon Valdez incident, and the events preceding it, prompted Exxon, now ExxonMobil, to develop and implement a safety program that has proved successful in preventing accidents. The system, known as the Operations Integrity Management System, has proved to be a reliable, if not highly routinized, approach to safety in an inherently volatile industry (Coll, 2012). Rex Tillerson, CEO of ExxonMobil, was asked to comment on the Exxon Valdez oil spill and its effect on how the company approaches safety. He explained that the accident had such an impact on the operations of the company, its reputation, and its perceived integrity that it required the company to take comprehensive actions to prevent an accident on the scale of Valdez from happening again. The mistake that led to the disaster resulted from a breakdown on several levels—leadership, operations, and even regulations. Much of what happened was due to the mindset of the company and operational safety systems. The Operations Integrity Management System at ExxonMobil now serves as the industry standard (Rose, 2013). The system seems to work: Exxon has yet to experience a major public breakdown since implementing the system.

CONCLUSION

The goal of this book was to open a window and explore how learning theory, research, and practice can inform the study of organizational resilience. By revisiting the roots of experiential learning theory as described by Dewey, we can begin to rethink how Dewey's vision of learning from experience can inform contemporary study and practice in organizations. Building on Dewey, the book offers a way of thinking about organizations as systems of interrelated learners, in which routines and novelties interact to form learning—and performance-based outcomes. In addition, a new language that removes the negative connotation associated with failure and replaces it with a language of learning and breakdown offers a new way to think about how organizations build resilience. By looking at various ways that learning can break down, we can begin to see how to sustain the natural tendency that most organizations have to learn. Popular management practices such as goal setting and rational thinking have their place, but often conspire to limit learning and can, when unchecked, threaten resilience. Future thinking on the topic of organizational learning and resilience are needed and should begin as this book did: by looking at how direct experience can lead to educative experiences. Only when direct experience serves as the basis for learning can educative experiences be realized.

REFERENCES

Advance Research Inc. (1965, October). *Critical industry repair analysis: Petroleum industry.* Washington, DC: Office of Civil Defense, Department of the Army. Retrieved from http://www.dtic.mil/dtic/tr/fulltext/u2/482909.pdf

Airbusdriver.net. (2012). *Airbus flight control laws.* Retrieved from http://www.airbus-driver.net/airbus_fltlaws.htm

Akerloff, G., & Shiller, R. (2010). *Animal spirits: How human psychology drives the economy, and why it matters for global capitalism.* Princeton, NJ: Princeton University Press.

Akhtar, S. (1996). "Someday..." and "if only..." fantasies: Pathological optimism and inordinate nostalgia as related forms of idealization. *Journal of American Psychoanalytic Association, 44,* 723–753.

Allison, P. T., & Zelikow, D. (1999). *Essence of decision: Explaining the Cuban missile crisis.* New York, NY: Longman.

Ameli, P., & Kayes, D. C. (2011). Triple-loop learning in a cross-sector partnership: The DC Central Kitchen partnership. *The Learning Organization, 18,* 175–188.

Aten, K., Nardon, L., & Steers, R. M. (2009). Rethinking the role of management development in preparing global business leaders. In S. J. Armstrong & C. V. Fukami (Eds.), *The Sage handbook of management, learning, education, and development* (pp. 497–513). Thousand Oaks, CA: Sage.

Audia, P. G., Locke, E. A., & Smith, K. A. (2000). The paradox of success: An archival and laboratory study of strategic persistence following radical environment change. *Academy of Management Journal, 34,* 837–853.

Baker Panel [Baker, J. A., III, Bowman, F. L., Erwin, G., Gorton, S., Hendershot, D., Levenson, N., Priest, S., Rosenthal, I., Tebo, P. V., Wiegmann, D. A., & Wilson, L. D.]. (2007). *The report of the BP U.S. refineries independent safety review panel.* Retrieved from http://www.bp.com/liveassets/bp_internet/globalbp/globalbp_uk_english/SP/STAGING/local_assets/assets/pdfs/Baker_panel_report.pdf

BEA [Bureau d'Enquêtes et d'Analyses pour la Sécurité de l'Aviation Civile]. (2012). *On the accident on 1st June 2009 to the Airbus A330-203 registered F-GZCP operated by Air France flight AF 447 Rio de Janeiro—Paris. Final Report.* Retrieved from http://www.bea.aero/en/enquetes/flight.af.447/rapport.final.en.php

Becker, G. S., & Murphy, K. M. (2001). *Social economics: Market behavior in a social environment.* Cambridge, MA: Harvard University Press.

Berg, N., & Gigerenzer, G. (2010). As-if behavioral economics: Neoclassical economics in disguise? *History of Economic Ideas, 18*(1), 133–166.

Best, R. A. (2005, December 2). *U.S. intelligence and policymaking: The Iraq experience* (Congressional Research Report for Congress RS21696). Washington, DC: Library of Congress. Retrieved from http://www.fas.org/sgp/crs/intel/RS21696.pdf

Bluedorn, A. C., Turban, D. B., & Love, M. S. (1999). The effects of stand-up and sit-down meeting formats on meeting outcomes. *Journal of Applied Psychology, 84,* 277–285.

Bowen, M. (2012, November). The hunt for Geronimo. *Vanity Fair, 627,* 145–194.

Briner, R., Denyer, D., & Rousseau, D. M. (2009). Evidence-based management: Concept cleanup time? *Academy of Management Perspectives, 23*(4), 19–32.

Burke, M. J., Salvador, R. O., Smith-Crowe, K., Chan-Serafin, S., Smith, A., & Sonehs, S. (2011). The dread factor: How hazards and safety training influence learning and performance. *Journal of Applied Psychology, 96*(10), 46–70.

Burnette, J. L., Forsyth, J. M., & Pollack, D. R. (2011). Leadership in extreme contexts: A groupthink analysis of the May 1996 Mount Everest disaster. *Journal of Leadership Studies, 4*(4), 29–40.

Campbell, D. J. (1988). Task complexity: A review and analysis. *Academy of Management Review, 13,* 40–52.

Cascio, W. F. (2007). Evidence-based management and the marketplace for ideas. *Academy of Management Journal, 50,* 1009–1012.

Central Intelligence Agency. (2002, October). *Iraq's weapons of mass destruction program* (declassified white paper). Washington, DC: Author. Retrieved from http://www2. gwu.edu/~nsarchiv/NSAEBB/NSAEBB129/nie_first%20release.pdf

Central Intelligence Agency and Defense Intelligence Agency. (2003, May 28). Iraqi mobile biological warfare agent production plants. Retrieved from http://www2. gwu.edu/~nsarchiv/NSAEBB/NSAEBB80/wmd32.pdf

Cheney, R. B. (2002). Vice President speaks at VFW 103rd National Convention. Retrieved June 22, 2008, from http://www.whitehouse.gov/news/releases/2002/08/20020826.html

Clegg, S. R., Courpasson, D., & Phillips, N. (2006). *Power and organizations.* Thousand Oaks, CA: Sage.

Cohan, P. (2012, July 13). Why stack ranking worked better at GE than Microsoft. *Forbes.* Retrieved from http://www.forbes.com/sites/petercohan/2012/07/13/why-stack-ranking-worked-better-at-ge-than-microsoft/2/

Cohen, M. D. (2007). Reading Dewey: Reflections on the study of routine. *Organization Studies, 28,* 773–786.

Coll, S. (2012). *Private empire. ExxonMobil and American power.* New York, NY: Penguin Press.

Commission on the Intelligence Capabilities of the United States Regarding Weapons of Mass Destruction. (2005, March 31). *Report to the President of the United States* (Silberman Robb Report). Retrieved from http://www.gpo.gov/fdsys/pkg/GPO-WMD/pdf/GPO-WMD.pdf

Committee of Privy Counsellors. (2004, July 14). *Review of intelligence on weapons of mass destruction* (The Butler Review). London, UK: The Stationery Office. Retrieved from http://webarchive.nationalarchives.gov.uk/20100807034701/http://archive.cabinetoffice.gov.uk/butlerreview/report/report.pdf

Conway, L., Suedfeld, P., & Tetlock, P. E. (2000). Integrative complexity and political decisions that lead to war or peace. In R. Wagner & D. Christie (Eds.), *Handbook of peace psychology* (pp. 66–75). Hillsdale, NJ: Lawrence Erlbaum Associates.

Crossan, M., Mauer, C., & White, R. E. (2011). Reflections on the 2009 Decade Award: Do we have a theory of organizational learning? *Academy of Management Review, 36,* 446–460.

Cyert, R. M., & March, J. G. (1963). *A behavioral theory of the firm.* Englewood Cliffs, NJ: Prentice-Hall.

Daft, R. L., & Weick, K. E. (1984). Toward a model of organizations as interpretation systems. *Academy of Management Review, 9*, 284–295.

Day, D. V. (2010). The difficulties of learning from experience and the need for deliberate practice. *Industrial and Organizational Psychology, 3*, 41–44.

Day, D. V., & Zaccaro, S. J. (2004). Toward a science of leader development. In D. V. Day, S. J. Zaccaro, & S. M. Halpin (Eds.), *Leader development for transforming organizations* (pp. 383–396). Hillsdale, NJ: Lawrence Erlbaum Associates.

De Oliveira, B. A. (2009). Book review of *Destructive goal pursuit: The Mount Everest disaster*, Palgrave-Macmillan, 2006. *Journal of Applied Christian Leadership, 3*, 67–76.

Dewey, J. (1938). *Experience and education.* New York, NY: Simon & Schuster.

Dixon, N. (1999). *The organizational learning cycle.* Aldershot, UK: Gower.

Doerr, T. (2004, May 26). *Oral testimony to the National Committee on Vital and Health Statistics.* Retrieved from http://www.ncvhs.hhs.gov/040526p1.htm

Drogin, B. (2007). *Curveball: Spies, lies and the man who caused a war.* New York, NY: Random House.

Drogin, B., & Goetz, J. (2005, November 20). How U.S. fell under the spell of 'Curveball'. *Los Angeles Times.*

Drumheller, T. (2006). *On the brink.* New York: Carroll & Graf.

Earley, P. C., Connolly, T., & Ekegren, G. (1989). Goals, strategy development, and task performance: Some limits on the efficacy of goal-setting. *Journal of Applied Psychology, 74*, 24–33.

Easterby-Smith, M. (1997). Disciplines of organizational learning: Contributions and critiques. *Human Relations, 50*, 1085–1113.

Edmondson, A. (1999). Psychological safety and learning behavior in work teams. *Administrative Science Quarterly, 44*(2), 350–383.

Eichenwald, K. (2012a). *500 days: Secrets and lies in the terror wars.* New York, NY: Touchstone.

Eichenwald, K. (2012b August). Microsoft's lost decade. *Vanity Fair.* Retrieved from http://www.vanityfair.com/business/2012/08/microsoft-lost-mojo-steve-ballmer

Elkjaer, B. (2001) The learning organization: An undelivered promise. *Management Learning, 32*, 4, 437–452.

Endsley, M. R. (1995). Toward a theory of situation awareness. *Human Factors, 37*, 32–64.

Ericsson, K. A., (2009) (Ed.). *Development of professional expertise.* Cambridge, UK: Cambridge University Press.

Ericsson, K. A., & Lehmann, A. C. (1996). Expert and exceptional performance: Evidence of maximal adaptation to task constraints. *Annual Review of Psychology, 47*, 273–305.

Erikson, E. (1956). "The problem of ego identity". *Journal of the American Psychoanalytic Association, 4*, 56–121.

Federal Aviation Administration. (2012). *Lessons learned from transportation airplane accidents.* Retrieved from http://lessonslearned.faa.gov/

Feith, D. J. (2002, September 16). *Assessing the relationship between Iraq and al Qaida.* Retrieved from http://www.levin.senate.gov/imo/media/doc/supporting/2007/SASC.Feithslides.040507.pdf

Feith, D. J. (2008). *War and decision: Inside the Pentagon at the dawn of the war on terrorism.* New York, NY: Harper.

Feldman, D. C. (1994). The development and enforcement of group norms. *Academy of Management Review, 9*, 47–53.

Fiol, C. M. (1994). Consensus, diversity, and learning in organizations. *Organization Science, 5*, 403–420.

Fishbach, A., & Choi, J. (2012). When thinking about goals undermines goal pursuit. *Organizational Behavior and Human Decision Processes, 118*, 99–107.

Foreign Policy. (2011). *The FP top global thinkers 2011.* Retrieved from http://www.foreignpolicy.com/articles/2011/11/28/the_fp_top_100_global_thinkers

Fraher, A. L. (2004). "Flying the friendly skies": Why US commercial airline pilots want to carry guns. *Human Relations, 57*, 573–595.

Garland, H., & Conlon, D. E. (1998). Too close to quit: The role of project completion in maintaining commitment. *Journal of Applied Social Psychology, 28*, 2025–2048.

Garvin, D. A., & Roberto, M. A. (2001). What you don't know about making decisions. *Harvard Business Review, 79*(8), 108–116.

Gelber, D., & Bach, J. (Producers). (2006, April 23). A spy speaks out. *60 Minutes* (broadcast program).

Gioia, D. A., & Thomas, J. B. (1996). Identity, image, and issue interpretation: Sensemaking during strategic change in academia. *Administrative Science Quarterly, 41*, 370–403.

Goffman, I. (1959). *The presentation of self in everyday life.* London, UK: Penguin.

Gorman, S. (2006, January 29). Little-known contractor has close ties with staff at NSA. *Baltimore Sun.* Retrieved from http://articles.baltimoresun.com/2006-01-29/news/0601290158_1_saic-information-technology-intelligence-experts

Graen, G. B. (2009). Educating new management specialists from an evidence-based perspective: A proposal. *Academy of Management Learning and Education, 8*, 255–258.

Gray, J. H., & Densten, I. L. (2007). How leaders woo followers in the romance of leadership. *Applied Psychology: An International Review, 56*, 558–581.

Greenwald, R. (Producer). (2004). *"Uncovered": The war on Iraq.* Canoga Park, CA: Cinema Libre.

Hardern, R. D. (2012). The 4-h target: An example of destructive goal pursuit. *Emergency Medical Journal, 29*, 219–221.

Harris Interactive. (2006, July 21). *The Harris Poll #57. Belief that Iraq had weapons of mass destruction has increased substantially.* Retrieved from http://www.harrisinteractive.com/vault/Harris-Interactive-Poll-Research-Iraq-2008-11.pdf

Head, B. W. (2008). Three lenses of evidence-based policy. *Australian Journal of Public Administration, 67*(1), 1–11.

Holliday, K. (2013, July 25). Goldman CEO on risk: The worst 'absolutely will happen.' *CNBC.* Retrieved from http://www.cnbc.com/id/100915696

Holman, D., Pavlica, K., & Thorpe, F. (1997). Rethinking Kolb's theory of experiential learning: The contribution of social constructivism and activity theory. *Management Learning, 28*, 135–148.

Hoover, J. D., Giambatista, R. C., & Belkin, L. Y. (2012). Eyes on, hands on: Vicarious observational learning as an enhancement of direct experience. *Academy of Management Learning and Education, 11*, 591–608.

Hunt, D. (1987). *Beginning with ourselves.* Cambridge, MA: Brookline Books.

Ibarra, H. (1999). Provisional selves: Experimenting with image and identity in professional adaptation. *Administrative Science Quarterly, 44*, 764–791.

Intelligence and Security Committee, House of Commons. (2003, September). *Iraqi weapons of mass destruction—intelligence and assessments.* London, UK: The Stationery Office. Retrieved from http://image.guardian.co.uk/sys-files/Politics/documents/2003/09/11/1109isc.pdf

Isaac, A., Shorrock, S. T., Kennedy, R., Kirwan, B., Andersen, H., & Bove, T. (2002). *Technical review of human performance models and taxonomies of human error in ATM*

(HERA). Brussels, Belgium: European Air Traffic Management Program. Retrieved from http://www.eurocontrol.int/sites/default/files/content/documents/nm/safety/technical-review-of-human-performance-models-and-taxonomies-of-human-error-in-atm.pdf

James, W., & Kuklick, B. (1980). *Pragmatism*. Cambridge, MA: Hackett.

Janis, I. L. (1972). *Victims of groupthink*. Boston, MA: Houghton Mifflin.

Janis, I. L. (1982). *Groupthink: Psychological studies of policy decisions and fiascoes*. Boston, MA: Houghton Mifflin.

Johnston, R. (2005). *Analytic culture in the U.S. intelligence community: An ethnographic study*. Washington, DC: Center for the Study of Intelligence. Retrieved from https://www.cia.gov/library/center-for-the-study-of-intelligence/csi-publications/books-and-monographs/analytic-culture-in-the-u-s-intelligence-community

Jones, J. M. (2003, February 6). *No signs of major impact from Powell speech*. Gallup News Service. Retrieved from http://www.gallup.com/poll/7747/Signs-Major-Impact-From-Powell-Speech.aspx

Kahneman, D. (2011). *Thinking, fast and slow*. New York, NY: Farrar, Straus & Giroux.

Kahneman, D., Slovic, P., & Tversky, A. (1982). *Judgment under uncertainty: Heuristics and biases*. Cambridge, UK: Cambridge University Press.

Kahneman, D., & Tversky, A. (1979). Prospect theory: An analysis of decisions under risk. *Econometrica, 47*, 263–291.

Kandel, E. R. (2012). *The age of insight: The quest to understand the unconscious in art, mind, and brain, from Vienna 1900 to the present*. New York, NY: Random House.

Kayes, A. B., & Kayes, D. C. (2011). *The learning advantage: Six practices of learning directed leadership*. Basingstoke, UK: Palgrave-Macmillan.

Kayes, D. C. (2002). Experiential learning and its critics: Preserving the role of experience in management learning and education. *Academy of Management Learning and Education, 1*, 137–149.

Kayes, D. C. (2004). The 1996 Mt. Everest climbing disaster: The breakdown of learning in teams. *Human Relations, 57*, 1236–1284.

Kayes, D. C. (2005). The destructive pursuit of idealized goals. *Organizational Dynamics, 34*, 391–401.

Kayes, D. C. (2006). *Destructive goal pursuit: The Mount Everest disaster*. Basingstoke, UK: Palgrave-Macmillan.

Kayes, D. C. (2009). Exploring performance versus learning in teams: A situation approach. In P. Kamur & P. Ramsey (Eds.), *Learning and performance matter* (pp. 137–156). Singapore: World Scientific Publishing Company.

Kayes, D. C., Allen, N., & Self, N. (2013). Integrating learning, leadership, and crisis in management education: Lessons from army officers in Iraq and Afghanistan. *Journal of Management Education, 37*, 180–202.

Kegan, R. (1998). *In over our heads*. Cambridge, MA: Harvard University Press.

Kerr, R., Wolfe, T., Donegan, R., & Pappas, A. (2004, July 29). *Intelligence and analysis on Iraq: Issues for the intelligence community* (The Kerr Report). Retrieved from http://www.gwu.edu/~nsarchiv/news/20051013/kerr_report.pdf

Kerr, S. (1995). On the folly of rewarding A, while hoping for B. *Academy of Management Executive, 9*, 7–14.

Kerwin, B., Balsa, G., & Taylor-Adams, S. E. (1997). CORE-DATA: A computerized error database for human reliability support. In *Global Perspectives of Human Factors in Power Generation, Proceedings of the 1997 IEEE Sixth Conference on Human Factors and Power Plants*. Washington, DC: IEEE.

Kim, J., & Miner, A. S. (2007). Vicarious learning from failures and near-failures of others: Evidence from the U.S. commercial banking industry. *Academy of Management Journal, 50*, 687–714.

King, P. M., & Kitchener, K. S. (1994). *Developing reflective judgment.* San Francisco, CA: Jossey-Bass.

Klein, G. (1999). *Sources of power.* Cambridge, MA: MIT Press.

Klein, G. (2008). Naturalistic decision making. *Human Factors: The Journal of the Human Factors and Ergonomics Society, 50*, 456–460.

Knight, D., Durham, C. D., & Locke, E. A. (2001). The relationship of team goals, incentives, and efficacy to strategic risk, tactical implementation, and performance. *Academy of Management Journal, 44*, 326–338.

Kolb, D. A. (1984). *Experiential learning.* Englewood Cliffs, NJ: Prentice-Hall.

Kranz, G. (2000). *Failure is not an option. Mission control from Mercury to Apollo 13 and beyond.* New York: Simon & Schuster.

Kurzweil, E. (1996). *The age of structuralism: From Levi-Strauss to Foucault.* New Brunswick, NJ: Transaction.

La Port, T. R. (2012). *Reprise of HRO developments: Reflections and future expectations.* Working Paper.

La Porte, T. (1988). The United States air traffic system: Increasing reliability in the midst of rapid growth. In R. Mayntz & T. P. Hughes (Eds.), *The development of large technical systems* (pp. 214–244). Boulder, CO: Westview Press.

Laqueur, W. (1999). *The new terrorism.* New York, NY: Oxford.

Latham, G. P., & Locke, E. A. (2006). Enhancing the benefits and overcoming the pitfalls of goal setting. *Organizational Dynamics, 35*, 332–340.

Laurendon, L., & Laurendon, G. (1997). *Paris catastrophes.* Paris, France: Parigramme.

Lawrence, P., & Lorsch, J. (1967). *Organization and environment.* Boston, MA: Harvard Business School.

Lerner, J., & Tetlock, P. (1999). Accounting for the effects of accountability. *Psychological Bulletin, 125*, 255–275.

Levin, C. (2004, October 21). *Report of an inquiry into the alternative analysis of the issue of an Iraq–al Qaeda relationship.* Retrieved from http://www.levin.senate.gov/imo/media/doc/supporting/2004/102104inquiryreport.pdf

Lewis, M. W., & Dehler, G. E. (2000). Learning through paradox: A pedagogical strategy for exploring contradictions and complexity. *Journal of Management Education, 24*, 708–725.

Locke, E. A., & Latham, G. P. (1990). *A theory of goal setting & task performance.* Englewood Cliffs, NJ: Prentice-Hall.

Locke, E. A., & Latham, G. P. (2009). Has goal setting gone wild, or have its attackers abandoned good scholarship? *Academy of Management Perspectives, 23*, 17–23.

Mandel, D. R., Hilton, D. J., & Catellani, P. (Eds.). (2005). *The psychology of counterfactual thinking.* London, UK: Routledge.

March, J. G. (1988). Decisions and organizations. Oxford, UK: Basil Blackwell.

March, J. G. (1991). Exploration and exploitation in organizational learning. *Organization Science, 2*, 71–87.

March, J. G. (2011). *The ambiguities of experience.* Ithaca, NY: Cornell University Press.

March, J. G., & Simon, H. A. (1958). *Organizations.* New York, NY: Wiley.

March, J. G., Sproull, L. S., & Tamuz, M. (1991). Learning from samples of one or fewer. *Organization Science, 2*, 1–13.

McLaughlin, J. (2008a, April 28). *Lessons from the search for Iraqi weapons of mass destruction.* Presented at the Security Policy Forum, The George Washington University Elliott School of International Affairs, Washington, DC.

McLaughlin, J. (2008b, April 30). Interview conducted by the author.

McLaughlin, J. E. (2005, April 1). *Statement of John E. McLaughlin, former deputy director of central intelligence.* Retrieved from http://www.fas.org/irp/offdocs/wmd_mclaughlin.html

Menand, L. (2001). *The metaphysical club.* New York, NY: Farrar, Straus & Giroux.

Mezirow, J. (1991). *Transformative dimensions of adult learning.* San Francisco, CA: Jossey-Bass.

Michaels, E., Handfield-Jones, H., & Axelrod, B. (2001). *The war for talent.* Cambridge, MA: Harvard Business Review Press.

Mihailovich, D. (Producer). (2007, November 4). Curveball. *60 Minutes.* Retrieved from http://www.cbsnews.com/video/watch/?id=3450752n

Mihailovich, D. (Producer). (2011, March 13). "Curve Ball" speaks out. *60 Minutes.* Retrieved from http://www.cbsnews.com/video/watch/?id=7359532n

Miller, D. (1996). A preliminary typology of organizational learning: Synthesizing the literature. *Journal of Management, 22,* 3 485–505.

Miner, A. S., Bassoff, P., & Moorman, C. (2001). Organizational improvisation and learning: A field study. *Administrative Science Quarterly, 46,* 304–337.

Miner, J. B. (2002). *Organizational behavior: Foundations, theories, and analysis.* New York, NY: Oxford University Press.

Miner, J. B. (2003). The rated importance, scientific validity, and practical usefulness of organizational behavior theories: A quantitative review. *Academy of Management Learning and Education, 2,* 250–268.

Mintzberg, H. (1979). *The structuring of organizations: A synthesis of the research.* Englewood Cliffs, NJ: Prentice-Hall.

Mintzberg, H. (2004). *Managers, not MBAs: A hard look at the soft practice of managing and management development.* San Francisco, CA: Berrett-Koehler.

Mogford, J. (2005). *Fatal accident investigation report. Isomerization unit explosion: Final Report. Texas City, TX.* Retrieved from http://www.bp.com/liveassets/bp_internet/us/bp_us_english/STAGING/local_assets/downloads/t/final_report.pdf

Mohr, L. B. (1982). *Explaining organizational behavior: The limits and possibilities of theory and research.* San Francisco, CA: Jossey-Bass.

Montagne, R., Butler, R., & Kelly, M. L. (2002, August 1). NPR analysis: Whether the U.S. should go to war with Iraq and the cost of such a mission. *NPR Morning Edition* (broadcast program). Retrieved from http://www.npr.org/programs/morning/transcripts/2002/aug/020801.kelly.html

Moran, M. (2012). *The reckoning: Debt, democracy and the future of American power.* New York, NY: Palgrave-Macmillan.

Morrell, K. (2008). The narrative of 'evidence based' management: A polemic. *Journal of Management Studies, 45,* 613–635.

Morris, M. W., & Moore, P. C. (2000). The lessons we (don't) learn: Counterfactual thinking and organizational accountability after a close call. *Administrative Science Quarterly, 45,* 737–765.

Mulford, C. W., & Comiskey, E. E. (2002). *The financial numbers game: Detecting creative accounting practices.* New York, NY: John Wiley & Sons.

National Security Archive. (1995–2004). *Saddam Hussein sourcebook: Declassified secrets from the U.S. Iraq relationship.* Retrieved from http://www2.gwu.edu/~nsarchiv/special/iraq/

National Transportation Safety Board. (2012). *Aviation statistics report. Table 5: Accidents, fatalities, and rates, 1992 through 2011.* Retrieved from http://www.ntsb.gov/data/table5_2012.html

Nelson, R. R., & Winter, S. G. (1982). *An evolutionary theory of economic change.* Cambridge, MA: The Belknap Press of Harvard University Press.

Nonaka, I. (1994). A dynamic theory of organizational knowledge creation. *Organization Science, 5,* 14–37.

Nutt, P. (2002). *Why decisions fail.* San Francisco, CA: Berrett-Koehler.

Ordonez, L. D., Schweitzer, M. E., Galinsky, A. D., & Bazerman, M. (2009a). Goals gone wild: The systematic side effects of overprescribing goal setting. *Academy of Management Perspectives, 23,* 6–16.

Ordonez, L. D., Schweitzer, M. E., Galinsky, A. D., & Bazerman, M. (2009b). On good scholarship, goal setting, and scholars gone wild. *Academy of Management Perspectives, 23,* 82–87.

Orton, D. J. (2000). Enactment, sensemaking and decision making: Redesign processes in the 1976 reorganization of US intelligence. *Journal of Management Studies, 37,* 213–234.

Palmer, R. E. (1969). *Hermeneutics.* Evanston, IL: Northwestern University Press.

Paulson, H. M. (2010). *On the brink.* New York, NY: Hachette Books.

PBS. (2006). The dark side. *Frontline* (broadcast program). Retrieved from http://www.pbs.org/wgbh/pages/frontline/darkside/

Perrow, C. (1999). *Normal accidents.* Princeton, NJ: Princeton University Press.

Peterson, C. (2000). The future of optimism. *American Psychologist, 55,* 44–55.

Pfeffer, J. (1993). Barriers to the advance of organizational science: Paradigm development as a dependent variable. *Academy of Management Review, 18,* 599–620.

Pfeffer, J., & Sutton, R. I. (2006). *Hard facts, dangerous half-truths, & total nonsense.* Cambridge, MA: Harvard Business School Press.

Pillar, P. R. (2003). *Terrorism and U.S. foreign policy.* Washington, DC: Brookings Institution.

Pillar, P. R. (2006, March/April). Intelligence, policy, and the war in Iraq. *Foreign Affairs, 85*(2), 15–28. Retrieved from http://www.foreignaffairs.com/articles/61503/paul-r-pillar/intelligence-policyand-the-war-in-iraq

Pillar, P. R. (2008). Interview conducted by the author.

Polyani, M. (1974). *Personal knowledge: Towards a post-critical philosophy.* Chicago, IL: University of Chicago Press.

Post, J. M. (Ed.). (2003). *The psychological assessment of political leaders.* Ann Arbor, MI: University of Michigan Press.

Post, J. M. (2004). *Leaders and their followers in a dangerous world.* Ithaca, NY: Cornell University Press.

Powell, C. (2003, February 6). *U.S. Secretary of State Colin Powell's presentation to the U.N. Security Council on the U.S. case against Iraq.* Retrieved from http://www.cnn.com/2003/US/02/05/sprj.irq.powell.transcript

Priest, D., & Arkin, W. M. (2010, July 21). The secrets next door. *Washington Post.* Retrieved from http://projects.washingtonpost.com/top-secret-america/articles/secrets-next-door

Probst, G., & Raisch, S. (2005). Organizational crisis: The logic of failure. *Academy of Management Executive, 19,* 90–105.

Rapport, L. J., Todd, R. M., Lumley, M. A., & Fisicaro, S. A. (1998). The diagnostic meaning of 'nervous breakdown' among lay populations. *Journal of Personality Assessment, 71,* 242–252.

Rasmussen, J. (1982). Human errors: A taxonomy for describing human malfunction in industrial installations. *Journal of Occupational Accidents, 4,* 311–333.

Reagans, R., Argote, L., & Brooks, D. (2005). Individual experience and experience working together: Predicting learning rates from knowing who knows what and knowing how to work together. *Management Science, 51,* 869–881.

Reason, J. (1990). *Human error.* New York, NY: Cambridge University Press.

Reay, T., Berta, W., & Kazman-Kohn, M. (2009). What's the evidence on evidence-based management? *Academy of Management Perspectives, 23*(4), 5–18.

Ribbens, B. A. (1997). Organizational learning styles: Categorizing strategic predispositions from learning. *International Journal of Organizational Analysis, 5,* 59–73.

Richou, G. (1895, November). The accident at the Montparnasse train station. *La Nature, 1171,* 369–371.

Robinson, M. D., & Ryff, C. D. (1999). The role of self-deception in perceptions of past, present, and future happiness. *Personality and Social Psychology Bulletin, 25,* 596–608.

Rose, C. (2013, March 9). *Interview with Rex Tillerman, CEO ExxonMobil.* Bloomberg TV Producers.

Ross, J., & Staw, B. M. (1993). Organizational escalation and exit: Lessons from the Shoreham nuclear power plant. *Academy of Management Journal, 36,* 701–732.

Ross, N. & Tweedie, N. (2012). Air France 447: 'Damn it, we're going to crash.' *The Telegraph.* April 28th, 2012. Available at http://www.telegraph.co.uk/technology/9231855/Air-France-Flight-447-Damn-it-were-going-to-crash.html

Rousseau, D. M., & McCarthy, S. (2007). Educating managers from an evidence-based perspective. *Academy of Management Learning and Education, 6,* 84–101.

Rudman, W. B., Parker, R. P., Oh, A. Y. K., & Kramer, D. J. (2006, February 23). *A report to the Special Review Committee of the Board of Directors of Fannie Mae.* Retrieved from http://www.concernedshareholders.com/CCS_FannieMaeReport.pdf

Rynes, S. (2007). Let's create a tipping point: What academics and practitioners can do, alone and together. *Academy of Management Journal, 50,* 1046–1054.

Scharf, R. H. (1998). Experience. In M. C. Taylor (Ed.), *Critical terms for religious studies.* Chicago, IL: University of Chicago Press.

Schulz, L. E., & Bonawitz, E. B. (2007). Serious fun: Preschoolers play more when evidence is confounded. *Developmental Psychology, 43,* 1045–1050.

Schulz, L. E., Goodman, N. D., Tenebaum, J. B., & Jenkins, A. C. (2008). Going beyond the evidence: Abstract laws and preschoolers' response to anomalous data. *Cognition, 109,* 211–223.

Schweitzer, M. E., Ordonez, L., & Douma, B. (2004). Goal-setting as a motivator of unethical behavior. *Academy of Management Journal, 47,* 422–432.

Scott, K. (Director). (2010). Crash of Flight 447. *Nova.* Retrieved from http://www.pbs.org/wgbh/nova/space/crash-flight-447.html

Scott, W. R. (1995). *Institutions and organizations.* Thousand Oaks, CA: Sage.

Sears, R. L. (1985). A new look at accident contributors and implications of operational and training procedures. In *Proceedings of the Flight Safety Foundation, 38th International Air Safety Seminar,* Boston, MA.

Seijts, G. H., Latham, G. P., Tasa, K., & Latham, B. W. (2004). Goal setting and goal orientation: An integration of two different yet related literatures. *Academy of Management Journal, 47,* 227–239.

Select Committee on Intelligence, U.S. Senate. (2004, July 9). *Report on the U.S. intelligence community's prewar intelligence assessments on Iraq together with additional views* (Senate Report 108-301). Washington, DC: Government Printing Office. Retrieved from http://www.gpoaccess.gov/serialset/creports/iraq.html

Simon, H. A. (1976). *Administrative behavior: A study of decision making processes in administrative organizations.* New York, NY: Free Press.

Sitkin, S. B., See, K. E., Miller, C. C., Lawless, M. W., & Carton, A. M. (2011). The paradox of stretch goals: Organizations in pursuit of the seemingly impossible. *Academy of Management Review, 36,* 544–566.

Smiley, P. A., & Dweck, C. S. (1994). Individual differences in achievement goals among young children. *Child Development, 65,* 1723–1743.

Smith, D., & Elliott, D. (2007). Exploring the barriers to learning from crisis: Organizational learning and crisis. *Management Learning, 38,* 519–538.

Smith, D. M., Loewenstein, G., Jankovich, A., & Ubel, P. A. (2009). Happily hopeless: Adaptation to a permanent, but not to a temporary, disability. *Health Psychology, 28,* 787–791.

Sorkin, A. R. (2009). *Too big to fail.* New York, NY: Penguin.

Special Advisor to the Director of Central Intelligence on Iraq's Weapons of Mass Destruction. (2005, March). *Comprehensive revised report with addendums on Iraq's weapons of mass destruction* (Duelfer Report). Washington, DC: Government Printing Office. Retrieved from http://www.gpoaccess.gov/duelfer/

Staley, K. F. (1996). *The art of short selling.* New York, NY: John Wiley & Sons.

Staw, B. M. (1981). The escalation of commitment to a course of action. *Academy of Management Review, 6,* 577–587.

Stein, M. (2004). The critical period of disasters: Insights from sense-making and psychoanalytic theory. *Human Relations, 57,* 1243–1261.

Stinchcombe, A. L. (1990). *Information and organizations.* Berkeley, CA: University of California Press.

Sundstrom, E., DeMeuse, K., & Futrell, D. (1990). Work teams: Applications and effectiveness. *American Psychologist, 45,* 120–133.

't Hart, P., Stern, E., & Sundelious, B. (Eds.). (1997). *Beyond groupthink: Political group dynamics and foreign policy.* Ann Arbor, MI: University of Michigan Press.

Tenet, G. J. (2002, October 7). *C.I.A. letter to Senate on Baghdad's intentions.* Retrieved from http://www.globalsecurity.org/wmd/library/news/iraq/2002/iraq-021007-cia01.htm

Tenet, G. J. (2004, February 5). *Remarks on Iraq's WMD programs.* Presented at Georgetown University. Retrieved from https://www.cia.gov/news-information/speeches-testimony/2004/tenet_georgetownspeech_02052004.html

Tenet, G. J. (2007). *At the center of the storm: My years at the CIA.* New York, NY: HarperCollins.

Tetlock, P. E. (1994). Integrative complexity. In M. Hewstone & A. S. R. Manstead (Eds.), *Dictionary of social psychology.* Oxford, UK: Blackwell.

Tetlock, P. E., McGuire, C., Peterson, R., Feld, P., & Chang, S. (1992). Assessing political group dynamics: A test of the groupthink model. *Journal of Personality and Social Psychology, 63,* 402–423.

Tetlock, P. E., & Mellers, B. A. (2011). Intelligent management of intelligence agencies: Beyond accountability ping-pong. *American Psychologist, 66,* 542–554.

Tetlock, P. E., & Tyler, A. (1996). Churchill's cognitive and rhetorical style: The debates over Nazi intentions and self-government for India. *Political Psychology, 17,* 149–169.

Thaler, R. H. (1999). Mental accounting matters. *Journal of Behavioral Decision Making, 12,* 183–206.

Thomas, E. (2006). *The very best men: The daring early years of the CIA.* New York, NY: Simon & Schuster.

Turner, B. A. (1976). The organizational and interorganizational development of disasters. *Administrative Science Quarterly, 21,* 378–397.

Turner, M. E., & Pratkanis, A. R. (1999a). Twenty-five years of groupthink research: Lessons in the development of a theory. *Organizational Behavior and Human Decision Processes, 73,* 105–115.

Turner, M. E., & Pratkanis, A. R. (1999b). A social identity maintenance theory of group-think. *Organizational Behavior and Human Decision Processes, 73,* 210–235.

U.K. Joint Intelligence Committee. (2002, September). *Iraq's weapons of mass destruction: The assessment of the British government.* London, UK: The Stationery Office. Retrieved from http://www2.gwu.edu/~nsarchiv/NSAEBB/NSAEBB80/wmd11.pdf

Useem, M., Cooke, J. R., & Sutton, L. (2005). Developing leaders for decision making under stress: Wild land firefighters in the South Canyon fire and its aftermath. *Academy of Management Learning and Education, 4,* 461–485.

Vaughn, D. (1996). *The Challenger launch decision: Risky technology, culture, and deviance at NASA.* Chicago, IL: University of Chicago Press.

Vince, R. (1998). Behind and beyond Kolb's learning cycle. *Journal of Management Education, 22,* 304–319.

Vince, R. (2001). Power and emotion in organizational learning. *Human Relations, 54,* 1325–1351.

Vince, R., & Reynolds, M. (2004). *Organizing reflection.* London, UK: Ashgate.

Vogus, T. J., Sutcliffe, K. M., & Weick, K. E. (2010). Doing no harm: Enabling, enacting, and elaborating a culture of safety in health care. *Academy of Management Perspectives, 24*(6), 60–77.

Voss, B. (2012). Opinion: Why do planes still crash? *CNN Online.* Retrieved from http://edition.cnn.com/2012/07/05/opinion/opinion-voss-why-do-planes-crash/index.html?hpt=hp_mid

Wasmund, S., & Newton, R. (2012). *Stop talking, start doing.* West Sussex, UK: Capstone.

Weber, E. J., Mason, S., Carter, A., & Hew, R. L. (2011). Emptying the corridors of shame: Organizational lessons from England's 4-hour emergency throughput target. *Annals of Emergency Medicine, 57*(2), 79–88.

Weick, K. E. (1993). The collapse of sensemaking in organizations: The Mann Gulch disaster. *Administrative Science Quarterly, 38,* 628–652.

Weick, K. E. (1995). *Sensemaking in organizations.* Thousand Oaks, CA: Sage.

Weick, K. E., & Roberts, K. (1993). Collective mind in organizations: Heedful interrelating on flight decks. *Administrative Science Quarterly, 38,* 357–382.

Weick, K. E., Sutcliffe, K. M., & Obstfeld, D. (1999). Organizing for high reliability: Processes of collective mindfulness. *Research in Organizational Behavior, 21,* 81–123.

Whyte, W. H. (1952, March). Groupthink. *Fortune,* 114–117, 142, 146.

Wilensky, H. L. (1967). *Organizational intelligence.* New York, NY: Basic Books.

Wilkerson, L. (2007, December). Interview on his collaboration on WMD presentation at UN. In *The Israel Lobby, VPRO Backlight* (broadcast program of Dutch Public Broadcasting). Retrieved from http://www.youtube.com/watch?v=iwdsm-Oux4o

Wilkerson, L. (2008, May). Interview conducted by the author.

Wilson, K. A., Burke, C. S., Priest, H. A., & Salas, E. (2005). Promoting health care safety through training high reliability teams. *Quality and Safety in Health Care, 14,* 303–309.

Wilson, T. D. (2004). *Strangers to ourselves: Discovering the adaptive unconscious.* Cambridge, MA: Belknap Press of Harvard University Press.

Wise, J. (2011). What really happened aboard Air France 447. *Popular Mechanics.* Retrieved from http://www.popularmechanics.com/technology/aviation/crashes/what-really-happened-aboard-air-france-447-6611877

Wise, J. (2012). Air France 447 and the limits of aviation safety. *Popular Mechanics.* Retrieved from http://www.popularmechanics.com/technology/aviation/crashes/air-france-447-and-the-limits-of-aviation-safety-10487501

Woodward, B. (2006). *State of denial.* New York, NY: Simon & Schuster.

World Encyclopedia. (2012 online version). Oxford, UK: Oxford Reference.

Zook, L. R. (2011). *Leading beyond invincibility, group-think, and other catastrophic attitudes.* Paper presented at the Wilderness Risk Management Conference. Retrieved from http://www.nols.edu/wrmc/LeadingBeyondInvincibility-Zook

INDEX

rank and yank (stack ranking), 64–65
rank-based performance systems,
    destructive side of, 64–66
Rasmussen, J., 50
rat-in-a-cage protocol, xiii
rational decision making, 88, 89t, 90
Reagans, R., 5, 141
Reason, James, 27, 50
Reay, T., 91
rebuilding, as stage of breakdown, 58f, 59t
red teams, 125–126, 135
reflection, learning from, 11
reflection experiences, 8
reflective observation, in Kolb's
    model, 12, 13
resilience, learning as source of, xi–xvii
retrospective sensemaking, 90
Reynolds, M., 57
risk awareness practices, 141
Robert, David, 25, 26, 27, 28, 29, 30,
    31, 32, 37
Roberto, M. A., 87
Roberts, Karlene, 49
Robinson, Jim, 10
Robinson, Michael, 82
routine learning, 17t
routine(s)
    disengaged routines, 33
    importance of, 15, 16
    influences on organizational routines, 22
    intersection of with learning, 36
    intersection of with performance, 36
    and learnng, 16–17
    living routines, 33
    misconceptions associated with, 15
    negative consequences of, 33
    shifting from to novel, 17–18, 17t, 28
rule-based failure, 50
Ryff, Carol, 82

Salas, E., 57
scenario-based training, 58
Schaffer Consulting, 65
Scharf, R. H., 6–7, 13
Schulz, L. E., 20–21
Schweitzer, M. E., 74
Sears, R. L., 142
See, K. E., 75
Self, N., 58
self-correction training, 57

self-deception, 82–83, 137
self-regulation, 72
sensemaking, 90
"sharp edge of the knife" problem, 51
short selling, 66–67
short-term performance orientation, 138
Silberman-Robb report, 129–130n44
Sitkin, S. B., 75
situational awareness, 95
60 Minutes (TV show), 124
SK Group Consulting, 46
skill-based failure, 50
Skilling, Jeff, 61, 62, 63, 64
slow decision making, 6
Smith, D., 57
Smith, D. M., 82
social identity theory, 80–81
social interaction phase (of learning), 14
Sportgevity, 141–142
stack ranking (rank and yank), 64–65
Standard Oil fire (1955) (case example), ix,
    138, 145
Standard Oil of Indiana, 145
standards of behavior, 28
Stasi (East German intelligence
    service), 107
Stern, E., 43
Stinchcombe, A. L., 16
stop rules, 96
Straw, Jack, 122
structure–nonstructure debate, 13
Sundelious, B., 43
Sutton, L., 16–17, 20
system coordination, failure of, 44t

task characteristics, 79
task complexity, 79
task coupling, 48
task duration, 79
task outcomes, 79
task structure, 79
teams
    ad hoc teams, 28–29, 133
    project teams, 28
    red teams, 125–126, 135
technology
    as core ingredient of failure, according
        to normal accident theory, 48
    reliance on at expense of
        experience, xv

Tenet, George, 103, 105, 118, 120, 121, 122, 123, 126

Tetlock, Phillip, 51–52

t'Hart, P., 43

Thompson, Morley, 66

Tillerson, Rex, 148

tough questions, 28

trade-offs, 52

tradeoffs, 96

Trailblazer project (NSA), 79

training interventions, 57–58

transformational learning, 11

trial and error, 20–21

Turner, B. A., 46–48, 58, 138

Ubel, P. A., 82

unbelievability, xiv

uncertainty, as threatening effectiveness of routines, 16

unintended consequences, 42, 52, 55, 68, 69, 72, 74, 76*t*, 77, 78, 78*f*, 79, 87, 96, 97

United Kingdom, emergency medicine in (case example), viii, xvi, 72, 138

unrealistic performance standards, vii

UN Security Council, 122

UN Special Commission on Iraq (UNSCOM), 103

U.S. Central Intelligence Agency (CIA), 101, 102, 103, 104, 105, 107, 110, 111, 112, 113, 114, 115, 116–117, 118, 121, 123, 125, 126, 133, 134, 138–139

U.S. Department of Defense, 107, 112, 115, 116, 117, 118

Useem, M., 16–17

U.S. federal aviation system (case example), ix. *See also* commercial aviation

U.S. intelligence community (case example), viii, xv, 132–133, 135, 138. *See also* weapons of mass destruction (WMD) in Iraq, CIA and intelligence community assessment of (case example)

U.S. National Transportation Safety Board, 142

U.S. Senate, 105

U.S. Senate Select Committee on Intelligence, 105, 114

U.S. State Department, 118

variability, as threatening effectiveness of routines, 16

Vaughn, D., 136, 138

vicarious learning, 10

Vietnam War, as groupthink example, 41

Vince, R., 57, 136

Voss, Bill, 30, 31

vulnerability, of organizations, 45, 70

Vygotsky, Lev, 11

The War for Talent (Michaels, Handfield-Jones, Axelrod), 65

Weapons Intelligence, Nonproliferation, and Arms Control (WINPAC), 103, 104, 109, 111, 121, 133

weapons of mass destruction (WMD) in Iraq, CIA and intelligence community assessment of (case example), viii, xii, xv, xvii, 41, 101–127, 132, 135, 136–137, 139

Weber, E. J., 72

Weick, Karl, 49

Welch, Jack, 65

Westinghouse brakes, 70, 71

"what if," psychology of, 19

"what if" scenarios, 49

Whyte, W. F., 41

Wilensky, Harold, 45–46, 70, 132, 134, 135, 137, 139

Wilkerson, Larry, 117–118, 119, 120, 121, 122, 139

Wilson, K. A., 57

Wilson, Tim, 94

WINPAC (Weapons Intelligence, Nonproliferation, and Arms Control), 103, 104, 109, 111, 121, 133

WMD (weapons of mass destruction) in Iraq, CIA and intelligence community assessment of (case example). *See* weapons of mass destruction (WMD) in Iraq, CIA and intelligence community assessment of (case example)

worst-case scenarios, 96

Zelikow, D., 134

Zirndorf, Bavaria, 108